82648   E
                         77.4
Shimer   S5
                         1971
The scroungers

Date Due

APR 23 '74	SEP 10 '9?		
NOV 29 '77			
DEC 14 '77			
FEB 1 '79			
NOV 7			
OCT 30 '87			
NOV 16 87			
JAN 25 1989			
FEB 4 1993			

THE SCROUNGERS

The Story of
Prehistoric Americans

About the Book

The first American of 50,000 B.C. was a scrounger, a hard, lean eastern Asian who left his continent for better fare in the Americas. He had a few poor stone tools and a poke stick. He knew a little about fire and a lot about survival. He could eat almost any flesh. Some of the plant roots and fruits that made up his salads would have been turned down by the most enthusiastic vegetarian.

Using the findings of innumerable archaeologists, R. H. Shimer tells the exciting story of how mankind survived and improved his lot in the Western Hemisphere despite strange and ferocious beasts and cataclysms of nature. From the scroungers developed vast and diverse empires in the Americas. This is the absorbing saga of the roots and traditions of the American Indians before the Europeans came.

THE SCROUNGERS

The Story
of Prehistoric
Americans

by R. H. Shimer

with illustrations by the author

G. P. Putnam's Sons · New York

Contents

THE SCROUNGERS

A successful scrounger ate what he could find

THE SCROUNGERS 1

Fifty thousand years ago men had a number of ways of making a living. Some lived by hunting in groups. Others were food collectors, gathering plants and small animals in a seasonal pattern. But many early men did neither of these things. They did not develop the tools or the organization for hunting in bands and they did not follow the cycle of ripening plants. They learned to use the food that was immediately available to them. They scrounged for a living.

The first American was a scrounger—a hard, lean East Asian who left his continent for better fare in the Americas. He had a few poor stone tools and a poke stick. He knew a little about fire and a lot about survival. He could eat almost any flesh. Some of the plant roots and fruits that made up his salads would have been turned down by the most enthusiastic vegetarian.

The scrounger killed anything he could step on, pound to death, strangle, or stab with a stick. He grabbed what he could from the kills of the big Ice Age predators while he fought it out with the other scavengers for the leavings. Once in a while he found an opportunity to live easily on the land. Usually, he made his own opportunities.

Mastodon, mammoth, great lion, saber-toothed cat, bear, and wolf dominated the hemisphere. The man who came to live among them didn't compete at their level. His role was different. The coyote, the vulture, and the man fit into similar niches in Ice Age ecology.

Scientists are convinced that this scrounger was not a native American.

There were native American primates, the order of mammals to which man belongs. The lemur family lived here 50,000,000 years ago. Tarsiers, the first of our kind of primates, survived in the Americas until 35,000,000 years ago. Many kinds of monkeys developed in the Western Hemisphere. They are still very numerous in Central and South America.

Scientists have tried very hard to find fossil apes or the bones of premen in the Americas, but they have been unable to do so. Primate development seems to have stopped with the monkey family in ancient America. Man didn't appear until the late Ice Age. He was an immigrant, invading the New World with some other Asian animals.

Who was the first human immigrant to the Americas?

Scientists don't know exactly. They don't have any skeletons of the earliest Amerind, the name scientists use instead of "Indian." All they have are his tools, his camps, his fire pits, and his garbage dumps.

The best guess is that the earliest Amerind was *Homo sapiens* fully developed. He was not a primitive kind of man. There were physically primitive men in the Old World 50,000 years ago. Neanderthal Man lived in Europe and the Near East. Cro-Magnon Man was just getting a foothold in Europe. None of their remains has been found near the Amerind's migration route.

What kind of modern man was the Amerind scrounger?

We can be sure he did not belong to any distinct race. The human family had not separated into these groups yet. Ancient Amerinds would have had the characteristics of Australoids, Caucasoids, Negroids, and Mongoloids. They would not have resembled these people because they descended from them. Rather, they would have showed their physical traits because all peoples have come from men who looked more like brothers than they do now. All had common ancestors.

Fifty thousand years ago that ancestor would have been hard to label. He may have looked a little like the tribesmen who live in the Amazon region today. The Amazon people have been sòme of the most isolated Amerinds. They were less affected by later immigrations than other Amerinds. Some think they look like a very early Asian people called Proto-Australoids. All people have changed a great deal in so many thousands of years, so the resemblance will only be general.

The immigrant who came to the Western Hemisphere didn't bring much with him. He came from the region of Asia where the least advanced Ice Age tools have been found. His motive for coming must have been food, primarily. And no one should rule out the possibility that Ice Age man was any less adventurous than man is today. However, there is no reason to think that he was aware he was entering a world where man had never set foot.

He was able to cross to another continent because of an Ice Age phenomenon. There was a land bridge connecting Asia and Alaska.

Scientists call the Asian–American bridge "Beringia" because it stretched across water that is now part of the Bering Sea. Beringia is now under more than 100 feet of water.

Beringia appeared because of the glaciers.

The sea level was lowered during glacial times. There is only a certain amount of water on the earth. When a large amount of it freezes into ice and stays packed in one region, there is less liquid to wash around the rest of the earth. More land was exposed during the Ice Ages. Some of this land appeared as isthmuses between continents. Beringia was one of these.

Beringia was the most available route from the Old World. There were others. Man could have come to North America from Europe by using the ice floes in the North Atlantic. It would have been quite a feat, even for a tough scrounger. There isn't any proof that this did not happen, however. Neither can the idea of Atlantic island bridges be discounted, even if they have disappeared. The Aleutian Islands were a very unlikely route. The Aleutian chain is warmed by Pacific air currents now. It is free of ice most of the year. Fifty thousand years ago it was part of the North American glacial sheet. It would have been nearly impossible for the immigrants to find food, even if they could stand the cold.

There was no open-water boating so early in man's history. We can be practically certain that men didn't build any oceangoing craft and sail to the New World until nearly modern times.

Beringia's climate was not exactly congenial. It was part of the Alaskan tundra. Bounded by icy Arctic waters and cut by bitter winds, it was a wet, rolling plain with enough moss and dwarf trees to support birds, rodents, and even large herd animals. The scrounger survived on it, too, with a few tools and a few talents. He may not even have had much clothing

to protect himself. Even today scroungers live in cold
lands. The Onas and Yahgans of the freezing Tierra del
Fuego region often go naked in the snow.

Man probably came to northern Asia during one of
the interglacial lulls. When a new Ice Age began, the
glaciers began building up in the north and west. He
was cut off from Europe and Africa. Beringia was east
of him.

Before and during the last glacial period, the one
scientists call the Wisconsin, the scroungers crossed
Beringia and spread over North and South America.
They traveled from the Alaskan tundra to the Strait of
Magellan and from California to Florida. It may have
taken them 25,000 years to do it. The earliest evidence
of man in South America is 25,000 years old.

Glaciers covered most of the north country. They
had been building up, receding, and building up again
for 60,000,000 years. There were two ways to get
between the main ice sheets and move south. These two
corridors were not always open. One of them was east
of the Rocky Mountains and ran down to central North
America. The other one was much narrower. It lay
west of the Rockies, between the main ridge and the
coastal mountain ranges.

These passes through the glaciers must have been
cold, wet, harsh routes even when they were free of ice.
They could support life. There were trees. They were
a source of food for men and other animals and provided fire material.

The immigrants probably traveled in small family
groups, the way nomads do. We can be sure their
passage did not go unnoticed. The American continents
were filled with animal life. They were the home of
the greatest variety of mammals on earth. Many species

Southward migration of Ice Age Amerinds

Wild Dog

Horse

Great Lion

Giant Sloth

that spread to other parts of the world had begun in the Western Hemisphere. During the Ice Ages, many Old World animals migrated to the Americas.

The earliest evidence of man in the Western Hemisphere was found in the Mojave Desert in California. Fifty-thousand-year-old stone tools were uncovered at an ancient workshop site in the Calico Mountains. There are several hundred of these tools. Many of them are pointed and sharpened by breaking flakes from their edges. There are Calico scrapers, knives, and hammerstones.

There is no way to know exactly when Calico Man arrived in California or just how he made his living. But it could hardly have been any way other than by scrounging, considering his tools. There are no tools that were perfected for hunting large animals. There are no specialized plant-collecting or plant-processing

Camel

Giant Anteater

Mastodon

Sabertooth Cat

Howler Monkey

Some Native Americans and Longtime Residents

tools. They are of the generalized type of tools that are used by people who scavenge and gather food erratically.

Fifty thousand years ago southern California was a cool, grassy region. A great menagerie of Ice Age animals lived there. Hundreds of thousands of bones of these animals have been found at the La Brea tar pits. The tar pits are now inside the central part of the city of Los Angeles. The tar was once covered by water. Animals were caught in it when they came to drink. The imperial mammoth, teratornis (the Ice Age vulture), camels, great lion, saber-toothed cat, short-faced bear, giant sloth, straight-horned bison, and many smaller animals have been reconstructed from the bones. Squirrels and birds still get caught in the tar at La Brea.

Calico Man lived in the same world as the extinct La

Caribou

Wooly Mammoth

Wolf

Asian Bear

Man

Fox

Some Ice Age Immigrants

Brea animals. As far as we can tell, he avoided death in the tar pits. In spite of his poor toolkit, he did have human cunning. It was the same kind of mental gift that lets the coyote survive where the wolf can't.

The Ice Age immigrant to the Americas left traces of several kinds of scrounging. Scavenging was one of them.

Evidence of Amerind scavenging was found at Lewisville, Texas. Lewisville Man built his fires about 37,000 years ago. There are more than fifty species of ancient animals represented in the bones he left around his camp. There are no complete skeletons of large animals. Lewisville Man grabbed parts of the kills of the bold predators. He managed to have meals of horse flank, venison, camel brains, and mammoth haunch, the share of the wily scavenger. These were the feast meals. In between, and much more often, the meat for dinner was provided by snails, snakes, mice, and prairie dogs.

There was danger in the scavenging life. Death in the arms of a bear, on the fangs of a cat or wolf, or on the tusks of a mammoth was always threatening. A scavenger's life expectancy would have been short.

Plant and small animal collecting was less risky. The scrounger did this kind of foraging without plan, and he probably did more of it than he did scavenging. Roots, fruits, seeds, eggs, reptiles, and rodents remains are found in very early camps on both American continents. Many scroungers may have lived out their whole lives without ever getting near the game trails. A glimpse of a mammoth, a camel, a straight-horned bison, or a mastodon might have been a rare thing where they made their living.

Wherever he found himself, the scrounger had to be adaptable. It may have been his most important char-

Scavengers fight over the remains of a kill

acteristic. The moody climate of glacial times was hardest on species that were rigid in their habits. The scrounger could change from berry-picking to gopher-catching, depending on what was available.

Scroungers who lived near the game trails did do some hunting. Certainly Ice Age man had a taste for the flesh of big game. He didn't show the same inclination to go after it that the big game hunter of later times did. He did have a few tricks. One was picking off the very young, the very old, and the disabled members of a herd.

Twenty-three thousand eight hundred years ago, according to an accurate system of dating called carbon dating, Ice Age man did this kind of hunting in Tule Springs, Nevada. At that time, the Tule Springs area was a prairie with tall grass, thickets of bushes and trees, and a big lake for a water hole. Horses, deer, mammoths, and camels used the water hole. So did man. Remains of his campfires have been found there. There were two big camps at Tule Springs. Both of them had stone tools. The tools, like those at Calico and Lewisville, showed that the men who used them had no specialized skills. A chopper, some scrapers, and a few splinters of bone made up the toolkit.

The Tule Springs hunter must have got his game by luring animals away from the herd: a young colt, a lame mammoth, or a buck deer that had been wounded in a fight because he was past his prime. The animals were trapped and stunned with rocks. They could be finished off with more rocks and the poke sticks. They were butchered with the crudest stone knives. The carcasses were roasted over open fires. Every morsel was eaten. The bones were cracked to get out the last bit of nourishing marrow.

Hunting was at its best when the scrounger found a whole species of animal that was more helpless than he was. Thirty thousand years ago he found a species of mammoth that was dwarfed. The little mammoth lived on Santa Rosa Island, off the California coast. He was between four and six feet at the shoulder. He was so small that he could be run to exhaustion and stoned to death. It was a very good situation for the ancient Amerinds who found him.

In addition to a population of mammoths, the island had excellent foraging ground. It had the south-of-the-glaciers climate that produced thick plant growth. There were plenty of fruits and nuts. The scrounger could also catch crabs and abalone at the beach. There were fish in the streams.

Man and mammoth lived together on Santa Rosa Island for 13,000 years. Neither of them changed much. The mammoth continued to be dwarfed, and the man continued to use only a bare minimum of poor tools. What was the need for better tools? Santa Rosa Man could drop his victim with rocks that he picked up off the ground. He could cut up his meat with an abalone shell.

The story of man was not enriched by any saga of progress on Santa Rosa Island. There was no real progress between the first fire, which has been dated 29,659 years ago and those that appear when the mammoth was dying out. The dramatic element is in the strange cast of characters. No storyteller could dream up a wilder plot, an Ice Age man running down a dwarf mammoth on an island paradise just north of Hollywood.

Even in the Ice Age, Californians must have been a little more exotic than the rest of us.

Santa Rosa Man and dwarf mammoths

The scrounger left evidence of his scavenging, foraging, and hunting. He left something else.

Someone in Puebla, Mexico, 30,000 years ago sat down and scratched pictures of mastodons, tapirs, and ancient bison on a piece of mammoth bone. Juan Camacho, an anthropologist, found this earliest Amerind art in the Mexican desert in 1960. It is the most human of the fossil remains of the scrounger that we have. It let us know that he did not live by berries and gophers alone. He observed his world, and he had an urge to record what he saw.

About 16,000 B.C. Amerinds began to use a spear with a stone point.

The spear in the Americas may have developed from the poke stick the foraging scroungers used or the fending stick that was used against fellow scavengers.

By 14,000 B.C. there were three major adaptations that men made to the environments of the Western Hemisphere. Two were based on hunting, and a third was a development from the foraging tendencies of the early scroungers.

Man did not become the dominant animal overnight, in spite of these adaptations and the development of the spear. He continued to maintain a healthy respect for all life in his environment. He never did try to subjugate other animals. He was proud to be related, by ancestry, to the coyote, the bear, and the raven. It was never a reluctant admission when he expressed the link between himself and the others. It was a point of dignity.

Perhaps the Amerind attitude came from the fact that the Americas were the great showcase of the mammals. Perhaps it was because of man's own early role in the hemisphere. It wasn't a matter of humility, certainly. There isn't anything lowly about a scrounging life. What does it take, for instance, for a naked Tierra del Fuegan Yahgan—one of the last scroungers left on earth—to race up an icy cliff, strangle a sleeping bird, and bite off its head?

It is at least as heroic as the pose of the hunter.

Fire and noise were used to panic big animals

THE AGE OF ADAPTATION: 2

The Herd Hunters

The Amerinds who adapted to herd hunting ranged from the glaciers to the southern tip of the Americas, anywhere the big herd animals migrated. Between 14,000 B.C. and 8000 B.C. the most common herd animals were the proboscidians—the mastodons and mammoths—and the camels and horses.

The mammoth was probably the most sought-after. He provided a hunting band with a huge supply of meat.

There were four main groups of mammoths during the Ice Ages. All of them had descended from a specialized mastodon. Amerinds hunted the woolly mammoth on the tundra near the glaciers. The woolly mammoth was very distinctive. He had a back that sloped down sharply, a bulb of fat on his forehead, huge circular tusks, and a thick body that was covered with long, reddish hair. The imperial mammoth lived on the plateaus of North America. He provided even more meat. He may have been the bulkiest land animal that ever lived. A bull could weigh 20 tons. Two other mammoths stayed in the Eastern Hemisphere.

Great numbers of mammoths fell to Ice Age spears in the Americas.

Before spears were developed, it would have been

very hard to kill a mammoth even with the use of fire. Fire ringing was used. So was stampeding the animals over cliffs, building pitfalls for them, and cutting out weaker members of the herd.

Mammoths were very plentiful in the Western Hemisphere during the Ice Ages. The damp weather encouraged the growth of trees and bushes and provided the kinds of food they liked best. Mammoths were browsers rather than grazers on grass. Perhaps it is because they developed as an order before the grasses took root.

It would not have been difficult for a hunting party to find a mammoth herd if it kept close to the migration routes the herds used. The important thing was spotting one in the right position for a kill.

Such a sighting must have been made near Dent, Colorado, about 11,000 years ago. The evidence of a mammoth kill has been uncovered by scientists at this place. It is possible to reconstruct the methods involved in the hunt from this evidence. Imagination can fill in the rest of the outline.

Imagine an early morning at a small stream. The stream is one of many that feed into the great river, the Platte. A hunting party is camped nearby. A few members of the party are drinking from the stream. Others are acting as lookouts. There are always dangerous animals—big cats, wolves, and bear.

One of the lookouts sees a mammoth herd on the march. The herd has come from the forests along the banks of the Platte, where the animals have been browsing for several days. They are moving toward a fresh supply of leaves. They begin to climb toward a grove of trees at the top of an incline. The lookout can see that the incline ends in steep bluffs.

It is a perfect arrangement for a hunting party.

The lookouts alert the people in the camp. Men pick up their spears. Women light torches from their cooking fires and give them to the men. They take some for themselves. The whole population of the camp starts after the mammoths. The men and women, carrying their torches, run up the sloping ground. The children follow. The children's job is to make as much noise as they can. Ice Age children probably had lungs as strong as modern children. The mammoths quicken their pace. When they smell the smoke and see the blazing torches behind them, they begin to gallop. The hunters follow, driving them all the way to the top of the hill.

Finally, the only routes that are open to the mammoths are backward, into the noise and fire, or forward, over the cliff.

The bluff is sandstone. It is too steep and crumbling for a safe descent. The elephant clan has excellent balance. Their feet are built for narrow trails. Even for them the bluff is too difficult. They regard the route through the torches as impossible.

The herd leader tries to find footing just over the edge. She tests it with her trunk and decides to try to climb down. Others follow her example. They all slip. Huge bodies plummet over the bluff. Most of them survive the fall. They are injured, but they have the strength to get up and run away.

Some calves and one bull don't make it.

The hunters throw boulders down from the top of the bluff. They stun the mammoths. When the animals are unconscious, the hunters come down close and finish them off with spears.

The flint choppers are put into use for the butchering. Great pieces of hide are sliced off and put aside to be scraped. Chunks of meat are soon coming off the carcasses. The cooking fires are lit.

The feast lasts all day and all night. Every stomach is full. For days the hunters stay beside the carcasses. They eat every scrap of meat. When the sun begins to rot the flesh and give it a bad taste, the women simply cook it longer.

The tusks are cut out of the sockets, and the ivory is shared equally. No one man has performed any great act of heroism. So none should get any greater share of the trophies.

Spears, choppers, and scrapers were the early mammoth hunters' most important tools. Before 8000 B.C. Clovis-style points were the most common. They were named for Clovis, New Mexico, where they were first found. Most of them were flint, but other stone, as well as bone and ivory, was used. Clovis points are larger than most later spearpoints. The scars where the stone is fluted to make a channel for the spear shaft are quite short. Later toolmakers among the herd hunters could get the shape they wanted by whacking off one or a few flakes.

Clovis spearpoint and scraper

Tool improvement was vital as man adapted to the conditions in the Americas. An unusual tool was found in Cochise County in Arizona in 1967. It was near some mammoth bones. Some scientists who have examined it think that it is an Ice Age shaft wrench, used to straighten spear shafts. The tool is made of bone. There is a hole in one end of the bone. The hole is beveled all the way around. It does not show any wear. If it had been used as a hole for a thong, there would have been some marks. It was not used as a weight or a decoration but to straighten spear shafts. It is an advanced tool for Stone Age men.

Ice Age shaft wrench

Other mammoth kills were different from the one at Dent. At Clovis six mammoths fell to the hunters. The slaughter took place at a water hole. When it was discovered, some people guessed that the mammoths had been surprised by the hunters and had been panicked by the slippery footing. Elephant men don't think that this would have been very easy to do. They know that it is quite difficult to sneak up on any kind of elephant. More likely, it was the hunters who were surprised when they came down for a drink. Suddenly they found themselves face to face with a small herd of mammoths.

The hunters were hungry, more hungry than frightened. The site didn't offer any means of a kill except direct attack.

The main group of hunters held the mammoths at bay with screams and spear waving while one man ran in. He dodged the tusks and plunged his spear behind a mammoth's foreleg and into his heart. The process was repeated with the others until all the mammoths had spearpoints in vital spots.

Direct attack on huge animals is terribly dangerous, but even today primitive African and Indian hunters kill elephants this way.

The Clovis mammoths were butchered beside the water hole. After the butchering, there wouldn't have been much question about who got his choice of the ivory.

For many years scientists wondered how early Amerinds, with their wooden spears and stone spearpoints, could kill tough-skinned mammoths. They would have to be extremely accurate spear throwers to strike one of the few vulnerable spots. The Amerind was that skillful, and a mammoth kill site near Naco, Arizona, proves it. In 1952 a mammoth skeleton was discovered there. Eight spearpoints lay among the bones. The points were very close together. Every one of them had been aimed at the small Atlas vertebra, one of the few vulnerable spots in a full-grown mammoth. One of the points rested squarely on the vertebra.

A large number of mammoth kill sites and mammoth hunters' camps in Mexico and on the Great Plains date from between 10,000 B.C. and 9000 B.C. Many scientists believe this is because of a thaw period called the Two Creeks period. It lasted only 100 years, from 10,000 B.C. to 9900 B.C. The warm weather widened the corridor between the North American glaciers. The Amerinds who lived north of the corridor were encouraged to move southward. Those who had come across Beringia more recently and had not adapted to the tundra probably came in the greatest numbers.

The human population did not come from any new migration during the Two Creeks period. Beringia was flooded during the warm weather.

Mastodons were hunted in large numbers at this time, too. They were downed by hunters from Florida to California and in South America, where mammoths did not live.

Mastodons were the most ancient of the proboscidians left at the time of the glaciers. They lived inside and at the edges of the thick, dank Ice Age forests and browsed on the foliage of the fir trees.

Mastodons had flatter heads than mammoths. They carried them more horizontally. They had long, strong trunks and beautifully engineered tusks. They were thick and sharp and curved up at the ends.

Another old proboscidian, the gomphotherium, had two representative varieties in the New World about the time the Amerinds were hunting. We don't know if they fell to the hunters' spears. Besides mammoths, mastodons, and gomphotheria, there were also ancient true elephants in the Americas. Once again, there is no proof that they were hunted.

Frequently, a single mastodon was killed. Perhaps mastodons were so hard to kill that one animal was all the hunter could manage. It would have been hard to pursue a mastodon herd. The forest lands where they lived were places with treacherous bogs. They swarmed with insects. The Amerind herd hunter was an open ground man. Anyone who has spent any time in the Midwest lake country of North America during mosquito season will be in sympathy with the hunters' reluctance to go into the subglacial forests.

The forests of South America near the Andean glaciers were mastodon homes, too. The South America hunters killed them. Scientists have come across several kill sites.

There is evidence that the Argentine hunters went after an even more exotic animal, the toxodont. Toxodonts were one of the pyrotheres, an ancient order of mammals that had nearly been annihilated by invasions of North American predators before the Ice Age. The

Argentine toxodon hunter

toxodonts were huge piglike animals that roamed the Argentine pampas. They had little natural protection except their size. They had no. tusks. One toxodont could feed a good-sized Amerind band.

Spearpoints were found with toxodont bones in the nineteenth century, but scientists refused to accept the evidence at that time.

In Brazil, near Lagoa Santa, the herd hunters killed camels and horses. Sloths, which were not herd animals, were also on the Brazilian herd hunter's menu.

Horses and camels also provided steaks in North and Central America. There was a lot less risk for the herd hunter who went after these animals than for the mammoth hunters.

Most Ice Age horses that were hunted weren't much bigger than the modern types. Their heads were a little more zebralike, and they probably carried a layer of fat on their bodies, the way the mammoths did. There were many kinds of American horses. One variety in Texas was as big as any draft horse that has ever been developed. There were others that were as small as Shetland ponies.

The Amerind could have had as fine a stable of work and riding horses as man has ever possessed if he had managed to domesticate them. He didn't. Hunters are very singleminded. The horses, large and small, were viewed in terms of cutlets.

The camel didn't get any more consideration. He was big enough to have carried people and their belongings all over the plains, from the Arctic to the Argentine. In the Old World no draft animal has been so reliable. If the camel could have been preserved, he might have had great value in the time of heat and drought that followed the glacial age. But he ended up in the stewpot every time. Camel bones are among the most common remains of the Ice Ages. America may have been the original home of the camel, as it was of the horse.

The herd-hunting Amerinds were in the best position to see the potential of the horse and the camel. They ignored it. The herd hunter of the Andes pursued the guanaco. He also kept his mind on food. The guanaco was the ancestor of the llama and the alpaca. They were domesticated much later by Amerinds who weren't chiefly hunters but foragers.

The Andean guanaco hunters roved along the highland country of South America. Some scientists believe that it was the major highway at that time. The jungle growth on the east prevented easy movement. The deserts on the west coast encouraged foragers but not hunters. The Andean glaciers were confined to certain peaks, so traveling was best along the high plateaus. A string of camps with similar tools has been found on the highland route from Tierra del Fuego to Central America and northward.

None of the herd hunters were inclined to give up their nomadic ways as long as their supply of migrating animals lasted.

American camels

Between 9000 B.C. and 8000 B.C. that supply was threatened.

The big Ice Age animals began to die out. The decline in the mammoth population was the most noticeable. The camps and kill sites of the mammoth hunters became fewer and fewer after 9000 B.C. By 8000 B.C. there may not have been any mammoths of any variety south of the glaciers. The mastodons, which had survived as a species for 35,000,000 years, also left the stage. So did the western horse and camel.

It wasn't only the big animals and it wasn't only the herd animals that fell. The short-faced bear and a species of rabbit, the great lion and a toad, the ancient antelope and a wolf died out.

It was the time known as the Great Extinction.

A chain of events involving weather, volcanoes, a disease-carrying fly, and perhaps an overeager hunter was responsible. No one can say which factor began the process.

The weather at the end of the Ice Ages was very hard, but it had rarely been good in the 40,000 years preceding the extinction. An increase in snow or cold might have driven the animals southward, if that had been the only factor. A series of volcanic explosions as big as or bigger than any in modern times did occur in late Ice Age times. Mammoths in the far north were literally ripped apart by the eruptions.

Herding animals are very susceptible to communicable diseases like rabies. Only a carrier is needed. There were plenty of insects, rodents, and small carnivores in the Americas that could have performed the function. The bat, a notorious disease carrier, was an inhabitant of the hemisphere.

And there was man.

Of all the ancient people who had long residence in an area, the Amerinds were the least destructive of their environment. Still, the herd hunter was a special sort. He had little sense of conservation when he approached a diminished herd. If anything, he was more eager for large kills because his food supply had been limited.

Deep cold, volcanoes, disease, man—something upset the ecological balance. Even a minor event can do that. A molehill changes the topography of a meadow. Several small changes may result in a larger one. Soon animals, plants, soil, water, sunlight, and air are affected.

The Ice Age animals seem to have died out from south to north. The last of the mammoths may have turned north for some kind of safety at the glacier's edge. The herd hunters followed.

When the herd hunters reached the tundra, they came into contact with another hunting people, the tundrans. These were the Amerinds who had stayed north of the glaciers. The two groups lived together or near each other for a time. Their tools are mixed. They must have learned a lot from each other, but the herd hunter learned more. He arrived with a big, crude spearpoint, and he left with a smaller, finely worked one.

Even with better tools, the herd hunter needed a miracle if he was going to continue his nomadic life on the plains.

The miracle came.

It was in the form of a relative of the cow, the bison. Bison poured into the vacuum that had been created by the departure of mammoths, horses, and camels. For the first time, the bison took their stand on the

Ancient straight-horned bison

plains of North America. The herd hunters pursued them very much as they had the mammoth.

The bison had come from the woodland areas that the Ice Age herd hunter had avoided. He wasn't like the modern "buffalo." This bison was the straight-horned variety. He was not as enormous as a mammoth, but he could have been almost as destructive when he charged. His ancestor, who had migrated from Asia, had been even bigger and more powerful than he. The earlier bison had died out in the Great Extinction.

Sometimes bison were tricked into falling over cliffs. Sometimes they were trapped by fires in box canyons. Sometimes they were attacked directly. Scientists have found many bison kill sites. It was the discovery of the site at Folsom, New Mexico, that finally convinced American scientists that Ice Age man had really lived in the Western Hemisphere.

In 1926 a tough, lasso-swinging black cowboy named George McJunkin made this discovery. He had been riding through Dead Horse Gulch, a canyon near the town of Folsom. He noticed some bones sticking out of the side of an arroyo. Dismounting, he slid down to the place where they were embedded. He was curious about two things: why the bones were buried so deep, and why the "arrowhead" with them seemed so strange. McJunkin told a local banker about the bones. The banker got in touch with some museum people. When the bones were investigated, they were found to be those of the ancient straight-horned bison. The "arrowhead" was an Ice Age spearpoint. It had been made by a man who lived 10,000 years ago.

The Folsom point, which had probably developed in the north, was used by herd hunters after 8000 B.C. The Folsom point was fluted to fit a spear shaft, as the Clovis point had been fluted by the mammoth hunters. The Folsom point was smaller and had a better tip and edge. The fluting was obtained by striking off one or a few flakes.

Folsom points

A typical Ice Age bison hunt took place at Big Sandy Creek, Colorado, over 8,000 years ago. A bison herd was trapped in a gulch. The bison were stoned and then speared to death. There were thirteen bison. The Amerind hunters threw the bones down into a pit as they did their butchering. Scientists have been able to figure out just how the butchering was done. The hunters were very orderly. The same routine was used for

Spear with atlatl

each carcass. None of the tail bones went into the pit. The bison hides were probably taken in one piece, with the tail attached.

Hunters who had attacked mammoth directly did not hesitate to charge into a bison herd. The hunter had a better spear to use, too. Sometime near the end of the Ice Ages, the spear thrower, or atlatl, was invented. An atlatl is a wooden shaft about two feet long. The hunter holds it on his hand. At the other end of the shaft there is a groove or hook. The spear shaft fits into it. The added length of the atlatl shaft gives the hunter's arm much more power because his leverage is increased. When the spear is cast, the atlatl stays in the hunter's grasp. Sometimes there is a leather thong that helps him to hold it.

The miracle lasted as long as the glacier did. When the plains warmed and then grew hot and dry, the grass burned off. The straight-horned bison died or migrated back to the damp woodlands, where other varieties of bison still lived.

For a while antelope were hunted successfully by the herd hunters. They were hard to catch. The giant antelopes of earlier days might have been better game. The modern type was nervous and very agile. It was difficult to get within spear-throwing range. Furthermore, there was very little meat on the antelope.

The pronghorn antelope continued to survive even when the plains got hotter and hotter. Pronghorns have hair that is made up of pithy air cells which act as a protective layer against temperature extremes.

Antelopes could not provide a basis of life for people who had lived off mammoths, horses, camels, and bison in the past. When the bison deserted the plains, the heart went out of the hunter. Possibly he had been the greatest hunter who had ever lived. His hunting skills, the length of his treks, and the number and size of the animals he killed have never been equaled. The European Ice Age hunters were mere foraging butchers compared to him.

He moved eastward, after the retreating bison. His

identity was lost among the people of the woodlands. It was thousands of years before man and bison returned to the renewed grasslands.

When they did, it was another man and a different bison.

Tundrans hunted the woolly mammoth

THE AGE OF ADAPTATION: 3

The Tundra Hunters

Many scroungers adjusted to tundra life instead of taking the corridors south to the plains. Sometimes the North American glaciers touched or almost touched, and there was no chance to travel south. These were the very times when it was the coldest, and Beringia was fully exposed. The influx of Asiatics was large.

Beringia wasn't a serious limitation on the tundrans, even when it was flooded. Tundrans form a circle around the frozen Arctic. They don't belong to one continent. They belong to the north. Each group does tend to stay in one latitude and develop its own characteristics, Reindeer people in Siberia, Lapps in Scandinavia, and Eskimos in Greenland and North America.

In ancient times the Asiatic immigrants adapted to a tundra that reached, in projections, much farther south than it does now. It included a large part of the Alaskan coast and Canadian lands that are forested now. The glaciers were its southern and eastern boundaries. Water that often froze was in the west. The top of the world was just north of the major concentration of tundra population in the Western Hemisphere.

The most important feature of any tundra is permafrost. Permafrost is the frozen soil that is constantly underground. Sometimes it is hundreds of feet deep. In summertime a few inches of top soil thaw. Patches of bright green appear. Plants bloom. There are splashes of yellow, orange, and red on the mossy ground. The plants are never very large. There are no normal-sized trees. Their roots can't push through the permafrost. Neither can ground water penetrate in the summer. When the sun melts the top layer of ice, there are lakes and pools all over the tundra. The land oozes. The winter is dark, and the cold is bitter. The wind whips along the level land with no hills to stop it.

A wet, treeless plain, bitter cold in the winter and filled with bogs and mosquitoes in the summer—who would want to live in a place like that!

The tundra hunter did. We know that tundrans were one of the most stable groups of people who inhabited the hemisphere. An ancient campsite at Onion Portage, Alaska, was used for thousands of years. So was one on the Firth River. Once the people had learned to live on the tundra and knew what its limitations were, they preferred it to any other environment. Even today, tundra people all over the north are miserable when they are forced to leave their desolate homes.

The barren look of the tundra is misleading. There is plenty of food for the plant-eaters. So there is plenty of flesh for the meat-eaters. The tundran was able to live as a hunter of big and small game without having to follow the herds. He stayed in areas where he knew the big animals—the woolly mammoth, the caribou, and the musk ox—had to pass.

The woolly mammoth lived in all the world's northern lands. He preferred the foliage at the edge of the glacier. He was smaller than the imperial mammoth of the Great Plains, but he was still one of the finest meat animals on earth. Woolly mammoths were numerous and traveled in large herds.

Because of the open nature of the country, it is possible that the tundrans had a harder time killing their prey. There were fewer natural traps like the one at Dent. Fire may have been used extensively. The tundrans may have developed techniques of cutting out part of a herd. Single and group kills of mammoths have been found, but it is hard for scientists to excavate in the frozen ground of the north.

A great part of the year, the tundrans had the advantage of cold weather to preserve their meat. They may have followed some system of caches in the permafrost, the way modern tundrans have done. If meat is buried deep enough and covered with sufficient rocks to keep out marauders, it will be as it is in a deep freeze. The

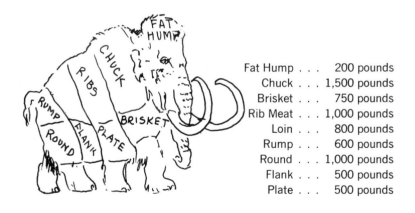

Fat Hump . . .	200 pounds
Chuck . . .	1,500 pounds
Brisket . . .	750 pounds
Rib Meat . . .	1,000 pounds
Loin . . .	800 pounds
Rump . . .	600 pounds
Round . . .	1,000 pounds
Flank . . .	500 pounds
Plate . . .	500 pounds

Estimated meat yield of a 16-ton bull mammoth

This estimate is based on a half-ton steer, with allowances for structural differences. It was estimated with the help of Bill Graham, head butcher for Stater Bros., Claremont, Calif.

woolly mammoth would have been the perfect animal for a food locker.

The range of mammoth migration on the tundra was probably hundreds of miles. The range of the musk ox was more limited, although it did move from summer to winter feeding grounds. Both mammoths and musk oxen were barren-ground tundrans. They did not go into the forests for food.

Musk oxen were mid-Ice Age immigrants to the Americas, like the caribou. They both crossed to Alaska for the cranberry, blueberry, crowberry, willow, small shrubs, and lichen that were thick on the American side.

Caribou are the great wanderers. The barren-ground caribou does not leave the tundra, however. There is a forest caribou that lives in the subarctic forest now. We don't know if he had any Ice Age ancestors.

Caribou must have been the most common game of the tundran, even though he may have preferred the mammoth. Caribou follow set rules of behavior even more than most other herd animals. They may use the same river crossing for thousands of years, even though they have been ambushed there frequently. The Onion Portage site indicates that tundrans often lay in wait at a shallow crossing of the Kobuk River. The river banks were thick with wild onion, which is a favorite food of caribou. There were salmon in the river to feed the hunting party while it waited. The hunters built their fires and roasted their game and fish at this place from early immigration times until the invading Eskimo penetrated the tundra. The tools of many different peoples and several major cultures have been found at Onion Portage.

Once again the Amerind had a chance to domesticate

a potentially useful animal. In some places, their reindeer cousins have been used as pack animals and milk producers and even as riding animals. To the tundran of the Western Hemisphere, he was nothing more than a meat animal. There was something in the Amerind makeup that allowed men to kill for food but not to use animals in other ways. The dog and the llama were the exceptions.

The tundran foraged for plants when he had to. In the Arctic, man and other animals regulate their lives by the cycles of the seasons, not by their own choice. Summer and winter, sun and darkness dictate what is

Spearing Ice Age caribou

to be done. Animals had to beware of the sudden freeze that could bring death. Some of them, like man, who had a limited amount of body fat, had to be careful about letting dampness accumulate on the skin during the cold weather. Some animals, men and bears, for instance, had to avoid boggy areas where their feet might trap them in the quagmires.

All of them had to watch out for the wolf.

The wolf of the Ice Ages has his counterpart in the Arctic wolf of today, although he wasn't more than a cousin. He was about the size of a modern wolf, but he had a bigger head, longer fangs, and a stockier body. Some of the best specimens of Ice Age wolf are found in the fine, black, sandy Alaskan mud that is called "muck."

Hungry wolves will attack almost any game, even a whole herd of musk oxen. The musk ox had a defense plan that may account for the survival of the species into modern times. The herd forms a tight circle with the bulls on the outside and the cows and calves in the middle. The bulls fight the wolves fiercely, with agility that doesn't seem possible for such a clumsy-looking animal.

The wolf was, and is, the only predator that can run down a full-grown caribou. He is fast and has tremendous endurance.

Another danger on the Ice Age tundra was the Alaskan lion. His remains have been found at such places as Rosey Creek, Alaska, just north of Fairbanks. The northern lion was very large, even compared to the great lion of the southwest United States. He had long fangs and, possibly, a striped coat like a tiger. A spearpoint has been found with the Alaskan lion remains uncovered at Rosey Creek. The human tundra hunter survived that encounter.

The bear was another Ice Age monster, but bear and man seem to have avoided each other in the Western Hemisphere. There are very few sites that indicate both mammals were present at the same time, and there is none that indicates an encounter.

The tundran and the wolf competed for the small game as well as for the large herd animals. Lemmings, weasels, and hares kept meat on the hunter's table when the musk ox, mammoth, and caribou were far away. Fish, birds, and eggs filled out the protein part of the diet. The tundra is filled with this kind of life. Some of the most choice game birds in the world live there. The fat tundra ptarmigan is one of the tastiest of all birds. He changes his color instead of migrating in cold weather, so that he is a constant food source. In season, there are geese, swans, and ducks for the tundra hunter. Bird darts were a useful tool, and they have been found in tundra camps, along with stone and bone spearpoints.

The tundra hunter didn't go after sea mammals as the Eskimo did later. This is not surprising. The tundran of ten or twelve thousand years ago was the descendant of a foraging-scavenging Siberian scrounger. He had no intention of taking to open water in a skin boat. He probably would have been willing to live on moose moss first. To remain a meat-eater he did not even have to get his feet wet except in the summer pools.

One of the things that distinguished the tundran from the herd hunter was his extremely fine, almost dainty spearpoints and cutting tools. They have been found in many places in the Arctic tundra lands. The fact that they do not appear in northern Asia makes most scientists believe that they were an Amerind tundra hunter invention.

The tundra hunter's precise tools may have been the finest stone tools of ancient times. Spearpoints were very thin and sharp. Both faces of the point, not just one, were worked to a fine edge. They might be bone, stone, or ivory. When they were made of stone, they could pierce flesh or carve better than anything except modern steel.

Bores for putting holes in hides, needles, and good scrapers were parts of the tool kit. They were more

Tundran sewing hides with bone needle

important in the Arctic than elsewhere. Hides were joined together by making holes in them and threading them with thongs. The hides were needed for clothing and shelter.

The tundra hunter had a unique role in ancient America. This probably began during the Ice Age. The tundran was a culture bearer. He was a selector of ideas from Asia and, perhaps, Europe. He was a transmitter of these ideas to the south. He also transmitted knowledge of his own tool-making skills.

The tundra hunters touched the domain of the herd hunters north of the Dakotas, at the foot of the corridors between the glaciers. On the extreme tip of the Wisconsin subglacial forest the tundrans also made contact with the foragers.

Perhaps there was intermarriage. Perhaps there was fighting. Certainly there was high excitement when one small group of Ice Age humans met another in the vast, dangerous world of early America.

A forager of the Adaptive period

THE AGE OF ADAPTATION: 4

The Foragers

The hunter lived according to the habits of the game animals. The forager adapted to the land. He followed the seasons. He didn't show the daring of the herd hunter or the hardiness of the tundran. Still, the forager fathered the planters of corn in Central America, the singers of hymns in the Andes, the builders of the mounds in Ohio, and the New World warriors of Mexico.

The trail of the foragers' camps leads directly to the most advanced Amerind cultures.

Foragers are not scroungers. At least, scrounging isn't their main occupation. Foraging is as specialized as hunting or farming. Special tools and special ways of gathering are needed. Each kind of foraging has to have its own tools and methods. Foraging bands were not usually limited by this, however. Foragers could change from one kind of foraging to another when they had to.

The herd hunters depended on one source of food, herd animals. They were in trouble when that source failed them. The tundra hunters depended on the persistence of one natural setting, the ecology of the tundra. It never did fail them. The tundra got bigger or smaller, but the hunters could always move with it.

Their life-style would have been destroyed if they could not have. Not the foragers. They could change from deer to fish or from seeds to snails if their situations changed. The meat went into the stewpot anyway, and the seeds made mush.

When the pickings were good, the forager knew how to process food and store it. No scrounger would have known how. When the pickings were slim, the forager knew how to stretch a meal. A hunter would not have. The hunter's cooking techniques didn't go much beyond the roasting stick. He knew very little about cooking plant food.

The climate of late glacial times often did an about-face. Ancient pollen from plants that grew in Colombia shows that between 10,500 B.C. and 8500 B.C. the climate changed from wet-cold to hot-dry and then to cold-dry. The Lake Mojave region of California had sudden changes from wet to dry and back again. These weren't like the changes between seasons. It meant that the whole ecology of a region was unbalanced. When that happened, the foraging people who lived in the area did not migrate. They substituted, invented, and survived.

There was more than one general kind of foraging life. What a forager did for a living depended on where he was living about 14,000 B.C., the time when most of the scroungers adapted to other life-styles. Today a person who lives on the California coast is more like one who lives in Arizona than he is like one who lives in Chile, regardless of how he makes his living. It was not always like that. Ten or twelve thousand years ago the Amerinds living near San Diego were more like those living at the Strait of Magellan than they were like those living in the Arizona desert. Their diets, their tools, and their living arrangements did not depend on latitude.

Any of them could have been picked out from the herd or tundra hunters by their semipermanent dwellings, their specific territories, their mixed diet, and their processing tools.

Four general types of foraging can be seen in the places where Adaptive foragers left traces of their lives. There were desert foragers, woodland foragers, plains foragers, and coastal foragers.

Just how did he do it? How did the forager become the only descendant of the scrounger who was completely adaptable? The answer is in the nature of his food collecting.

The forager was a data processor extraordinary, one of the world's most efficient.

For the forager, processing data meant gathering innumerable facts about nature and using them to his advantage. He hadn't drawn any better territory or had any more luck than the hunters as far as climate was concerned. His forest homes were wet and cold. His deserts seemed to be barren. The animals on the plains were just as elusive to him as to other early Amerinds. But he had learned how to discover the data —the facts of his environment—and how to manipulate them.

These facts had to be kept in the forager's own memory because he didn't have any written language. The data included thousands of bits of information. A forager living in the Tehuacán Valley of Mexico about 8,000 years ago, for instance, had to remember data on time, direction, and plant growth, at the very least. The number of facts and the way they were used would have made a respectable job for a modern computer.

Specific Territory	
Seasonal or Semi-permanent Dwellings	
Variety of Foods	
Large Tool Kit	Needles Weapon Points Cord Milling Equipment Choppers, Scrapers Knives, Hammers

Marks of the Forager

The Tehuacanos were desert foragers who lived in their valley many thousands of years, beginning sometime in the Ice Ages. Scientists have examined the caves around the Tehuacán Valley. These caves show what one of the earliest foraging life-styles was like.

A lot of Tehuacán data depended on the river in the valley. The Tehuacanos had to know when the river, the Río Salado, would flood the plain.

They had to know which autumn moon the deer would be in the oak grove in the eastern canyons and which autumn moon they would be in the lower hills. They had to remember what time the peccaries would be in the thorn forests. The people had to have some help keeping track of this time data. Perhaps they scratched marks on a stick, one mark for each nighttime moon and a larger one for each full moon. Sticks with data marks on them are called tally sticks. When they are used to keep track of nights and moons, they are calendars. Many primitive people have used the tally-stick method for calendars because it is hard to keep track of passing time.

Nature didn't make anything easy for the Tehuacanos. Plants did not ripen in a straight marching order. In the rainy season, when the Río Salado rose, mesquite pods were ready to harvest in the west and avacados in the east. There was cactus fruit in the east in the spring, and there were acorns in the canyons in the fall. It was back and forth and all around for the collecting Tehuacanos.

The early Tehuacanos had to have a lot of plant data. They had to know what part of the plant could be eaten. There are many toxic plants, some of them fatal, in the American Southwest and Mexico. The people also had to know how to harvest the fruit. Anyone who has ever reached too eagerly for a deep red prickly pear, without thinking about the cactus spines, will understand what that means. Needles seem to jump into fingers and wrists. Only the biggest ones can be pulled out. The others are embedded. They stay in and fester.

The habits of deer, peccary, jackrabbit, skunk, gopher, dove, and quail that lived in the valley had to be noticed and remembered.

Landmarks were data on directions. A hill, a brook, or a big rock might point out the direction of a march. The sun and stars helped. The stars in the clear desert sky were bits of information to early Amerind foragers, just as the habits of animals and plants were.

Besides all this data that the forager kept in his memory, the events of each day had to be considered. A baby was born. A sick grandfather needed extra water or special food. The dry season had been longer than usual. More acorn baskets had been made and the Tehuacano band wanted extra time to collect in the oak grove. These were things that altered the picture. They were new facts that had to be considered along with the data stored in the people's memories.

Other desert foragers faced similar problems in data processing. In our own Southwest there were foragers whom scientists have named Desert Culturists. They may have been the most advanced foragers in the Americas during the Age of Adaptation. Danger Cave, Utah, was one of their semipermanent homes. They returned to it season after season.

The Danger Cave people had millstones for grinding seeds. They made baskets for storing nuts and seeds. They plaited cords, made nets, wove hats to keep off the desert sun, processed rabbit fur into material for

Desert Culture woman milling seeds

clothing, shaped sandals with cord, made stone drills to start fires, and fashioned horn spoons.

These things were in addition to the making of tools like the hunting atlatl and the stone spearpoints. The deserts of the Ice Ages often had patches of grass and pools where the people did their hunting. The deserts themselves were much smaller than modern deserts. They were probably one of the most pleasant homes during that cold, wet time in man's history.

The Desert Culturists weren't the only people with such a rich tool inventory. Other desert foraging Amerinds were also processing seeds into flour by using millstones. By 7000 B.C. millstones were known in North, Central, and probably South America. For people who keep score, that's one point for the home team. People did not mill grain anywhere else in the world for two thousand years after the Amerinds started, as far as scientists know.

At first glance, it seems that the woodland foragers ought to have had an easier life than the people in other areas during the Age of Adaptation. There were ample food, more opportunity for shelter, and kindling wood for fires. Nowadays, when scientists explore the caves of the ancient Amerind woodland foragers, they seem like pleasant homes. Russell Cave in Alabama is a place like that. A stream of cool air runs from an opening at the back of the cave to its mouth. Ventilation is good on that hot Alabama hillside.

When the early foragers lived there, things were different. The pluvials, the rainy periods of glacial times, made the region wet and chilly. That draft of cool air from the back of Russell Cave was just a pain in the neck to some of the earliest Alabamans.

The Russellians hunted deer, bear, turkeys, raccoons,

rabbits, turtles, and snakes for food and pelts. Their tools were the kind that people use to clean small animal skins rather than the kind that are used for processing plants. They had baskets made from the reeds that grew in the streams instead of baskets made from yucca fiber. They had fine bone needles to sew the soft deer hides together.

Many of the earliest tools in Russell Cave are for woodworking. No desert foragers, even in the Ice Ages, would have wasted much effort making tools like that. Instead of the horn spoon that the Danger Cave people had, the Russellians had spoons made from shells of river shellfish.

The Midwest area of North America was the home of the Modocans. They were woodland foragers who lived at the Modoc Rock Shelter in Illinois.

The Modocans lived in the middle of deer country. There were so many deer that the people used their skins for blankets, bags, and rope as well as for clothing. Great piles of deer bones were left around Modoc.

It must have been possible to get sick of venison. The remains of other animals that were eaten at that time were also left in the garbage heap. The gnawed bones of rats, fish, and birds and the shells of turtles and clams were tossed out after Modocan suppers.

The Modocans had good stone axheads for woodcutting. Perhaps they even made the earliest dugout canoes to travel along the rivers that wound through the woods of the ancient Midwest. Dugout canoes can be fashioned with fire and woodworking tools such as those the Modocans left.

One of the earliest remains of human bones probably belonged to a Midwest forager. The skull of an Ice Age woman was found near Pellikan Rapids, Minne-

Woodland forager using a fire drill

sota. Many scientists believe that the skull is 10,000 years old. The skull is referred to as "Minnesota Minnie." An older skull, 12,000 years of age, came from Midland, Texas. It is also a woman's skull. It probably belonged to a member of a herd hunting band. It was found near Ice Age herd hunting camps. Extinct horses, antelope, and bison were nearby. The oldest skull of all those that have been found belonged to a man who was a plains forager in the West. It is 13,000 years old. The man whose skull was found is called Marmes Man because the find was made on the Marmes ranch in eastern Washington.

The Great Lakes forest region must have been an uncomfortable place to live during the Ice Ages. The glaciers formed the northern boundary. It was a spruce-fir jungle, expanding and contracting at the whims of the glacier. It was the real forest primeval. It may have been forested for millions of years, even before the grasses became common 25,000,000 years ago. The spongy forest carpet was made of moss and tree droppings. The sun that slanted through tiny openings between the spruce boughs barely warmed the air before night came.

There were plenty of meat animals in the forest. Mastodon, giant beaver, elk, caribou, deer, and even walrus and whale in Lake Huron offered a menu for the spearman. The fact that the foragers were not chiefly hunters is illustrated in this subglacial forest as clearly as it is anywhere. In Michigan alone there are thirty-six counties where mastodon remains have been found. There are twenty-three counties where the weapons of Ice Age man have been found. There is not one single tool in association with mastodon bones. Game could be just so big and take just so much effort for the forager. After that, he returned to his routine collecting.

The Great Lakes foragers certainly did prey on the smaller game animals, and they ate a lot of fish. Remains of their camps have been hard to find. This is not surprising. Glacial lakes swamped the area time after time, and the tracks of the foragers were almost obliterated.

Foragers' camps that date after 7000 B.C. have been easier to find. The glacier had begun its permanent retreat by that time. The mastodons had gone along. So had some of the foragers. They actually seemed to prefer life at the edge of the glacier. Pines and hardwoods took over the southern Great Lakes region.

The woodland foragers lived on the shores of the glacial lakes or on the islands. They must have had boats. They fished and hunted and gathered in a cycle that was dictated by the ice mountains to the north.

At Brown Valley, Minnesota, they showed that they were among the more sophisticated Ice Age people. They had progressed to a belief in an afterlife. They buried their dead with ornaments and tools for their use.

Some of the woodlands of South America were as cold and damp as those of the north. The Andean glaciers lasted almost as long as those in Canada. Most of the South American woodlands seemed to have been inhabited, however. Woodland foragers lived near the Pedregal River in 14,000 B.C. They left tool marks on the bones of animals that are now extinct. Foragers lived near Lake Maracaibo in 10,000 B.C. The ancient Maracaibos made some of their tools out of fossilized wood.

The South American woodland foragers had quite a

South American woodland foragers

menagerie to choose from when they went on their food-collecting expeditions. The forest animals had had better protection from the predators than the ancient animals on the South American plains. Mammals like the giant capybara, giant armadillo, anteater, giant sloth, and giant hog survived into modern or nearly modern times. The saber-toothed cat and the wild dogs that had penetrated South America when it had been rejoined to North America just before the Ice Age had less luck in the forests. They slaughtered whole species on the plains. The animals of the rivers and the deep forest held their own until the Great Extinction took them.

Monkeys, jungle birds, iguanas, tapirs, cavies, and toads also lived in the shady lands below the Andean glaciers. They were hunted the most frequently. The largest animal that seems to have been hunted with any regularity was deer. Apparently they were clubbed to death.

Cacao, zapote, and palm nuts filled out the larder of the woodland forager. They grew in the temperate and warm forests that were farther from the mountains. South American forests that later became steaming jungles were a lot more habitable from 14,000 B.C. to 5500 B.C. than they are now.

The plains foragers lived in territories that were crossed and recrossed by the herd hunters. Once in a while, when the forager made a lucky kill, they even ate the same game. The foragers didn't follow the herd, however. Their camps have the lived-in look of all camps of foraging people. They treated the herd animals the same way they treated the other data in their search for food. They certainly didn't abandon their planned existence to go chasing after mammoths.

If there is any confusion about which plains people were herd hunters and which foragers, their tools will straighten it out. If the tools are mostly spearpoints and scrapers for cleaning hides, then the people were probably herd hunters who had pitched camp for a short stay. If there are tools for processing small animal skins and plants, choppers, bores, needles, milling stones, and baskets, then the people were foragers, regardless of a camel bone or two.

The Taguans of Laguna de Tagua Tagua in central Chile are an example of South American plains foragers. They lived in big-game country. There were mastodons, horses, and probably glyptodonts and toxodonts in the earliest times of human habitation. The area was a plain surrounded by high mountains. It had only one narrow pass leading into it from the northwest. There was a lake on the plain. It made a good watering place for animals, including the wandering herds. At the site where the Taguans camped, they left mastodon bones—not a whole mastodon, by any means—deer bones, coyote bones, and horse bones. In much greater abundance are the remains of birds, frogs, fish, and rodents. They provided the bulk of the Taguan diet. It was supplemented by plants that grew around the lake and in the foothills of the mountains. Taguan tools, the implements that show us they were not scroungers, were often made out of horse bones. They were well-made tools. They may have been one of the chief reasons the foragers took the trouble to hunt horses.

Plainsmen were adept toolmakers, even if they were not so precise as the tundrans of the north. One clever tool that has turned up on the North American plains is the bola. Bolas are grooved balls that are held with cords. They are hurled at animals, especially birds, in an attempt to entangle their legs. If bolas are thrown correctly, the cords will hamper the flight of a bird or an animal. The quarry can be finished off with a dart or by hand if the hunter is fast enough.

Bolas were used in historic times on the Argentine pampa. Ancient bolas dating from 10,500 B.C. have been found in New Mexico and Nebraska. These plains

Hunting cranes with a bola

foragers may have been after whooping cranes. Whooping cranes were once very numerous in the Southwest. The bola is the perfect weapon to use against the long-legged crane.

Marmes Man, who contributed the oldest Ice Age skull yet found, was a plainsman who foraged. He hunted deer, coyote, and elk, which are not herd animals. Among the bones found near him, the only herd animal represented is the antelope. Scrapers and a very fine bone needle also found at Marmes identify the people as foragers who depended on their skill in processing skins.

There is a grim note at Marmes, too. Marmes Men may have hunted one another. There is some evidence of cannibalism.

Some of the plains foragers lived in the middle of mammoth and bison hunting territory. More than 10,000 years ago they had a semipermanent camp at Medicine Creek, Wyoming. From the kinds of garbage they left, it appears that they lived on the creek in the spring, the summer, and part of the fall.

The Medicine Creek people had milling stones and many bone foraging tools. They ate the flesh from prairie dogs, rabbits, rats, coyotes, and of course bison. They also seemed to have a peculiar liking for the larvae of mud dauber wasps. They baked the mud nests and then broke them open to get at the larvae. They must have been considered a great delicacy, considering the number of roasted nests that have been found.

Trading may have gone on between hunters and foragers on the plains. The mammoth hides which began to multiply in the hunter's camp would have been very desirable to the forager. Items of basketry, cord, and worked stone and bone would have been just as sought after by the hunters, whose long treks didn't leave them the leisure for such creations.

The remains of many coastal foraging camps have been lost to the tides and the changing shorelines of the hemisphere. Scientists have managed to find some of the sites where Ice Age men made a living by the sea, however.

Many of the coastal food collectors were still pure scroungers after 14,000 B.C., as they had been before. There was no pattern to their gathering. Others, especially on the Pacific coast of South America, were well-developed data processors. They disprove the old idea about beachcombing being the lowest form of human existence. Living off the sea and sand wasn't always an uncomplicated life-style. Many ancient Amerind foragers improved their lot with better tools and methods of fishing and gathering.

During Ice Age times there was a foraging group living in Peru, near the modern town of Ancón. The Ancón region has an unusual climate—even for Peru. It is (1) on the Pacific Ocean, so the air is moist, (2) cool and cloudy most of the year, and (3) one of the most arid deserts in the world. This seems like a contradiction, but it is the case. The last rain in Ancón was in 1925. Even at the time of the Ice Age pluvials, there wasn't much more rain than there is now.

This unusual combination of ocean air and desert flats made the lomas, green fog meadows. During glacial times these fog meadows were much larger than they are now. They may have been eight or ten times as big. They supported clusters of green plants. The only water they got came from the air. Millions of snails fed on the plants, and thousands of Ice Age Peruvians fed on the snails.

The foliage and the snails were on the lomas about seven months each year. The foragers camped there during that time. They harvested the snails and gath-

Gathering seeds and wild potatoes on the Peruvian lomas

ered seeds and a wild, bitter potato that grew there. Their diet also included burrowing owls, lizards, and deer and guanaco that came down from the mountains to feed on the lush lomas.

The rest of the year the Lomaseros spent at the water's edge. The current along the Peruvian shore is the cold Humboldt, a river in a warm sea. Plankton, those colonies of tiny plant-animals, were plentiful in the cold current. Fish, mussels, clams, sea lions, gulls, cormorants, and pelicans fed on the plankton and fell to the darts and stones of the Lomaseros.

By 8000 B.C. the Lomaseros were making tools to chop and strip plant fibers. They had millstones to grind the hard lomas seeds into flour, and they had stone sickles to help with the harvesting.

There was nothing revolutionary about the progress of the foragers. It was a steady thing. Each new invention was placed in the data inventory. It made life richer. It didn't change the foragers' life-style in any dramatic way. This holds true even for the discovery of seed cultivation in the next period of their history.

Compared to the Old World cultures of Egypt, Mesopotamia, and India that were developing at about the same time, the Amerind foraging communities begin to look positively primitive. The Old World people who had been harvesting wild seeds and grubbing for roots also changed radically when farming began. They drew themselves into an ordered society while the Amerinds, who had cultivated plants themselves, went right on living as fragmented clusters of people.

The Old World leaders could have had much more than the basic necessities even early in agricultural history, by 3000 B.C. at least. They wanted and they were able to get luxury and excitement in their lives. The monotony of the foraging cycle was over for them.

In the New World chiefs were seldom more than leaders of a hunting or collecting party.

The life-style in the Old World didn't provide luxury, excitement, and comfort for everyone. It didn't even provide food for all. It certainly did not offer freedom to most of the people. When the sudden civilizations of the Old World are considered from the slave's point of view, the slow foraging life looks good. The Amerind considered as rights the very things that became privileges so early in the Old World—a full stomach and a free soul. He may still have dressed in rabbit skin and scooped water with his hand, but he had independence.

Some of the foragers did follow the path to civilization once the seed was planted instead of gathered. Others, many others, continued to live in their old territories, cooperating with nature instead of trying to outwit her.

The length of the foragers' residence in some areas is remarkable.

The Lomaseros continued to make their camps on their weird fog meadows for more than 5,000 years. They were part of the coast's farmer-fisher communities after that for another 2,000 years. When the coast people were finally incorporated into the Andean religious unions, these people still maintained an independence of sorts.

The Russellians of Alabama inhabited their cave from 6200 B.C. until A.D. 1650.

Danger Cave shows a 10,800-year occupancy, from 9000 B.C. until A.D. 1800.

What was magnificent about the Amerind foragers was their shabby durability.

An archaic woodland forager fixes his harpoon

THE ARCHAIC
AMERINDS 5

A warm wind blew in from the east. The women came to the front of the cave and looked out at the stirring leaves. The men who were fishing in the stream and waiting for the usual morning drizzle talked about the wind. It was different from any they had ever felt.

It was a dry wind, and it was warm.

The warm, dry wind came again that year. The following year it came many times. It was the beginning of the altithermal, the drying time that finally ended the Ice Ages. It parched the Great Plains and extended the North American deserts. It shrank the Peruvian lomas by the sea, pushed the northern spruce forest onto the edge of the tundra, and made a paradise of the eastern woodlands.

The gloomy, gray forests with their icy rivers became temperate woods. Patches of sunlight filtered through the leaves and warmed the woodland air. The streams were glutted with shellfish. There were so many of them that children could harvest enough for whole families. The water was alive with fish. It was warm enough for wading.

The foragers began to move onto the riverbanks. The big caves, like Russell and Modoc, were still used, but they were probably winter shelters. The stream-bank communities became villages. They still were not permanent in the modern way of looking at things. The riverbank settlements were places where the people returned after foraging expeditions. These expeditions might take weeks or months. They could put up their bark wigwams on the old site, perhaps even on the hard soil of the old foundations.

The bumper crop of shellfish wasn't the only big addition to the woodland food supply. Every year there were more acorns and hickory nuts, blackberries and grapes. The browsers increased. Deer were plentiful. They were even thicker than during the Adaptive period. So were fat black bears. The bird population exploded. New ecological patterns were established. The close relationship between deer, turkey, and oak tree, each one a food or fertilizer for the other, was only one of these successful patterns. They lasted for many thousands of years, until the Europeans came and spoiled the forest.

Every living thing in the woodland seemed to profit from the sunshine.

Larger groups of people could forage together. Family groups became tribes. Knowledge about new tool developments could be passed from one neighbor to another. This is very important to people like fishermen. A fish trap can provide a lot more food than a fish spear. The Boston fish weirs, which were large fish traps, were set out near the present city of Boston in Archaic times. The Boston fish weir discovery was one of the finds that showed that man had a long history on the Atlantic coast as well as in the West.

The changing climate produced many new food sources. The foragers discovered them and enriched their diet. Many new and improved tools appear as a result. We find haft axes, chisels, adzes, bone fishhooks, darts, spears, and nets in the toolkit of the Archaic woodland forager. Many of the tools were almost modern in design.

Imagine an Indian summer day in the Archaic eastern woodland. A man sits in his cave with other men, women, children, and grandchildren of his family. A big fire burns in the cave. A meal is set on wooden platters and everyone feasts. The man eats steamed clams, a gumbo of wild rice and frog legs, roast breast of turkey, snapping turtle soup, spiced pumpkin, sassafras tea with drops of maple syrup, trout deep-fried in rich bear fat, tiny fresh blueberries from a basket, and to top off the meal, handfuls of butternuts, hazelnuts, and dried grapes. When a primitive family wanted a feast in those Archaic times, it would not use halfway measures.

After dinner the cave gets too warm. The man walks outside. He takes a trail through the kind of oak forest you'll never see. It leads to a brook where the water is so clean the sunlight glints off the stones on the bottom. The man stops for a drink. He lies down on the forest carpet and looks up through the leaves at a sky that is bluer than any you can imagine. He listens to the cooing of a passenger pigeon, a sound that you'll never hear.

This picture, with a different menu, could be repeated in other woodlands in North and South America.

In the North American Midwest the foragers had whole new areas opened to them. The glaciers had reached far down into the Great Lakes country. Now they had receded into the north. The foragers found new varieties of plants and new homes. They found something else—copper.

The Archaic Midwesterners of North America were

the first workers in metal in the New World. They were probably the first in the whole world. In the Upper Great Lakes region the Old Copper Culture appeared by 5556 B.C. This is the carbon date of the earliest known site that contains worked copper. The Old Copper people had the most advanced culture in the hemisphere before farming took hold in the South. They had a steady food supply and all the tools they needed to maintain a successful foraging schedule that allowed them to be almost completely settled. They had a standard of living that included art, religion, and ceremonial burial of the dead.

An Old Copper Culture craftsman

At first the Midwesterners must have thought that the copper was a kind of stone. It was lying on top of the ground the same way. They picked it up and worked with it the same way they did flint. It must have been quite a surprise to the first toolmaker who tried to break off a piece of copper with a hammerstone. The copper just changed shape. It didn't break at all. It could be beaten into any shape, even into sheets.

The pieces of copper that the people found on top of the ground were nearly pure. The only processing that was needed could be provided by a hammerstone. No smelting of any kind was attempted. Even after copper was mined by the Old Copper people at Isle Royale and on the Keweenaw Peninsula, they didn't really develop an art of metallurgy. Copper was never smelted or combined with other metals. It was just like a piece of wood or stone except that it would take new shapes more easily and it could be made to shine in the sunlight.

The miners of copper in the Midwest followed the veins of pure copper from the places where they showed on the surface. They dug pits around them. When the copper was embedded in rock, they built fires around the rocks and then threw cold water over them to make them crack. After this was done, the rock could be broken up with hammerstones and the copper recovered.

Some copper mine pits got to be 20 feet deep. The ore was hauled out in birchbark baskets.

Spearpoints, ax heads, daggers, fishhooks, and jewelry were made of copper. The people used it for personal decorations and in ceremonies. Even though many things were fashioned from it, copper remained a nov-

Mining copper in the Archaic Midwest

elty. No bronze age followed the introduction of copper. The people went right on living in their foraging communities, unaware of what metal could really do for them.

The Old Copper people kept at their work for several thousand years. It is very possible that they had learned about plant cultivation in the South about halfway through their history. They may have been farmers at the end of the time they appear as a distinct culture.

They would not have needed to be. They were very successful woodland data processors.

One thing can be said with certainty about the world of the Old Copper people. The data in the area were changing constantly.

The New World's first metal tools

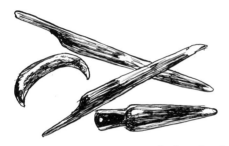

At the beginning of the Archaic period, when the Midwest was discovering copper, the level of the Great Lakes and other lakes in the area was hundreds of feet lower than it is now. During the following 3,000 years, the length of the Old Copper culture, the water level rose until it was hundreds of feet higher than today. There was less land to forage.

Earth heaves occurred. These happened when the weight of the glacier was removed and the compressed ground rose.

More important for relatively settled people, the region's whole ecology changed. The hot weather drove the pine forest northward. Then the hardwoods, the oak, and the chestnut came and went north. An ecology based on grass took over the southern and western parts of the Old Copper area.

Just as the Browns Valley foragers had followed the subglacial forest in the Adaptive period, many of the Archaic Old Copper people moved along with their familiar trees. A great number of them, in traditional forager fashion, stayed and coped with their environment.

Those who emigrated came into a new land. It had been freshly created, a gift of the glacier.

The northern boundary touched the tundra now, not the glacial ice. In the east the forests ran along hills and through river valleys. In the central northland the land was more level. There were many lakes. West of this was a cold extension of the Great Plains. The snow-capped, forested mountains rose beyond the plains. These highlands extended all the way to the Pacific coast. It was a fabulously beautiful country of spruce, pine, sea cliffs, and mountains.

Elk, beaver, lynx, cougar, moose, wolf, otter, deer, and bear multiplied in the old glacial lands.

During Archaic times the human population of the northern forest included the Midwestern immigrants, perhaps a few tundrans, and some important new people from the west. The newer element may have been moving into the continent slowly for a long time. They may have been coming since the final closing of Beringia, about 6000 B.C. Or they could have been an immigration of sea nomads from one of the Pacific rim territories. By Archaic times there were open-water sailors and ships capable of accomplishing the trip from Asia.

The mixture of peoples in the northern forests was the foundation of the Algonquin tribes.

The Algonquin foraged all over the north country. They built dugouts in Archaic times, and they used the bow and arrow for hunting. It was the most important weapon improvement since the development of the stone-tipped spear 15,000 years earlier.

An Algonquin archer

There was a considerable amount of contact and exchange of tools and ideas between the Algonquin and the people of the southern woodlands. Copper ornaments turn up in the north country, and fine tundran tools appear in the south. Some scientists think that the fishing equipment and the bone lamps that are in the Archaic level in Russell cave came from Arctic people.

The tundrans continued to live in their unique world. They had contacts with each other in the vast tundra. Similar tools have been found on different Archaic sites in the north. The tundrans had lived many thousands of years on the Firth River in the Yukon country. An American archaeologist, Richard MacNeish, and his crews have dug down and found many different levels of occupation. On the third oldest level there are tools like those the people of Denbigh made. Denbigh is far to the west. A little later, the tools at Onion Portage look like Denbigh tools, too.

The shrinking tundra limited the hunters more and more. The northern trees came nearer each year. By the end of Archaic times, places parallel with Cape Denbigh had lost their permafrost. The Yukon Valley had trees. Timberland encroached on Onion Portage. But there was still enough tundra to keep the hunter fed.

The tundrans had new neighbors who were pushing in from the west.

The Eskimo people had established themselves on the Arctic coast.

The origin of the Eskimos was considered a mystery for many years. Now scientists are fairly certain that they came from one of the sea hunting communities on the rim of the western Pacific. They probably originated in or near the Philippines.

Scientists who didn't have much evidence about the Adaptive tundra hunters used to think that the Eskimos were Alaskan or Siberian foragers who had taken to the sea. There wasn't any reason for them to do so, even in Archaic times. Some Eskimos did become tundrans after they made their homes on the Arctic shores. The techniques of tundra hunting and gathering could be learned by the newcomers, but sea-mammal hunting is another thing again.

The most essential items to the sea-mammal hunter of the north, the Eskimo, are the skin boat, the toggling —turning—harpoon head, and the oil lamp. This trio means survival on the Arctic coast. They must even spell contentment, considering the famous Eskimo disposition.

There was nothing like the skin boat in the north before the Eskimos came. No coastal site has any indication of one. The Siberians had wooden boats in which to hunt walrus and seal at the mouths of the Asian rivers that empty into the Arctic Ocean. The wood for the boats comes from the Siberian forests. The Arctic provides very little boat-building material. On the Alaskan side it is just as barren as on the Siberian.

The Siberian seal and walrus hunters never ventured out into the open water with their wooden boats.

The people of the south and central Pacific are great boat designers. They are also great travelers. It isn't hard to see several bands of them going north, hunting sea mammals for generations while they seek out the breeding grounds. They hunt near Japan. They learn many things. Eskimo art has many Japanese characteristics. The Eskimos follow the seal, the walrus, and the whale farther north. When they find the places where these mammals are plentiful, the Arctic Ocean, they stop. They spread along the Arctic coast, east and west.

Children trained to be sea mammal hunters

In the west they go only as far as the Kolyma River; the Siberian Sea is not good sea-mammal hunting territory. The coast of Alaska is much better.

The Eskimos settled in villages. From these spots they could exploit the sea for otter, fish, walrus, and seal. They could hunt the land behind them for bear, birds, and eventually caribou. They adapted to the Western Hemisphere at its northernmost edge. There isn't any indication that this was before 2500 B.C. Even in 2000 B.C. there were not many villages. They were all very distinctive. The Eskimo life-style on the coast has changed very little since then. It demands careful and early training of the children, division of adult labor, reliance on a good supply of fur and oil, and unchallenged social balance. Still, there has been time to develop a wonderfully complex art. People have often been surprised to find decorations on tools and pure art objects in a land where survival itself is such an effort.

About a thousand years after the Eskimos occupied the coastal edges of the tundra, one group of them split off and formed its own culture. These people became known as Aleuts. The Aleuts still have a strong language and physical similarity to the Eskimos, although time has blurred it. The Aleuts occupied the Alaskan Peninsula and the Aleutian Islands. The land was free of ice by that time. Even during late glacial times, the Aleutian Islands had inhabitants. The camps of Ice Age Adaptive foragers were found on Anangula Island.

The Aleuts absorbed this early population and started a life built on sea-mammal hunting like their Eskimo cousins.

The Arctic and the subarctic forest gained population. South and west of the forest, the Great Plains lost inhabitants. The territory was by no means abandoned.

Foragers continued to hold out after the herd hunters retreated to the east.

The Logan Creek people, who were Archaic Nebraskans, managed a standard of living that included stone fireplaces, milling, sewing, beadmaking, and some settled fishing villages on the small plains rivers. They left fine curved bone fishhooks along with their milling stones and sewing awls. They managed to bring down a few bison that are still a puzzle. These bison may have belonged to a type between the huge straight-horned bison and the modern type. They couldn't have been very numerous, and they certainly didn't provide a living for a hunting group.

Mussel shells were in good supply when the creek was running. Heaps of shellfish remains seem to have been the mark of Archaic people in America. Even the dry plains had them.

The Logan Creek people were in their Nebraska homes by 4676 B.C., and there is evidence that their camp was used by other people before them. The Logan Creek people stayed through the scorching years that followed, living on seeds and rabbits when the fishing gave out.

On the southern plains, in central Texas, the Edwards Plateau people kept up the foraging tradition. Beginning about 5000 B.C., they made their homes in caves and rock shelters and on stream terraces. They left their stone dart points, knives, scrapers, axes, choppers, and millstones scattered along the plateau. The axes suggest that there was some wood to cut. Small trees must have held out along the stream banks.

The Edwardians made jewelry of stones that they had polished. Again there was art where life would seem to have been too hard for the effort. A polished stone pendant hung from a rabbit-hide thong on some suntanned Edwardian girl's neck while she toiled at the millstone.

The Grove people of Archaic Oklahoma, the Fumerole people of Archaic New Mexico, and the Butte Dwellers of Archaic Nebraska were other plains foragers who processed data under the hot sun. The game became more and more meager: rabbits, a few deer, Archaic bison, an antelope, a prairie dog—all of them went into the Archaic plains stewpot.

In spite of the weather, seeds kept sprouting, ripening, drying, and dropping. In the Archaic period the Amerinds began to manipulate these bits of data that they knew so much about.

The Cochise Seed Gatherers of the North American Southwest were on the verge of sowing the seed as well as harvesting it for many centuries. They were the descendants of the Desert Culturists of the Adaptive period. These people, along with other desert foragers, had been the first Amerinds to concentrate on plant data.

The desert had expanded under the hot sun. There were still seasonal rains, and the streams did run for a short time during the year. There was enough moisture to sprout the seeds that had dropped from plants the year before. There were mesquite trees that seemed to be able to survive on a few teardrops.

Early in the year the plants grew on the riverbanks. After the water disappeared, there was still a little dampness in the stream beds. Smaller plants could grow there. The Cochise foragers lived along the river bottoms. They used as much of each plant as they could. Besides the seeds, they used the stalks as fibers for weaving.

Milling stones grew large. Spearpoints almost disappeared. Baskets grew big enough to store seeds for many months.

The Cochise Seed Gatherers followed the seasons and watched the seeds sprout, grow into plants, ripen their seeds, and drop them. They continued to search for them instead of trying to plant seeds for themselves. There is no reason to think that some of the desert plants couldn't have been cultivated by man. Corn itself is an open-country, hot-weather grass. It would have done very well in Texas, New Mexico, and Arizona, the Cochise people's territory. The ancient type of pod corn must have grown there.

In 1948 Herbert Dick, an American scientist, did find a piece of pod corn preserved in the choking dust of Bat Cave, New Mexico. It was dated 2500 B.C.

That was already midmorning in the history of corn culture in the Americas.

People were growing corn in the Tehuacán Valley by 5000 B.C. Those cactus-harvesting, peccary-hunting, avocado-eating Tehuacanos began to cultivate plants without causing more than a ripple in their foraging pattern. Certainly there were no waves. Corn was grown. Foraging continued.

Scientists have tried very hard to find the original corn from which the Amerinds developed their hundreds of varieties. The Amerinds who met Columbus called their plant "maize." It was much different from the "corn" of the Old World. Corn meant kernel, though, so the Europeans didn't see why corn shouldn't be classified with all grains. "Maize" became "corn," and it is too late to change people's minds about it.

Many scientists thought that *teocentli*, which is a plant that looks like corn, was the ancestor of modern

A Cochise picks senna pods; a rattlesnake disputes him

corn. Many of them tried to cultivate a modern variety from *teocentli*. They gave up. It was agreed that it would take 20,000 years of very scientific horticulture to develop it. Even Burbank tried to get corn from *teocentli*. He thought that he had done it. Then he found out that he hadn't started with *teocentli* at all but with a modern variety itself.

The closest thing to modern corn that scientists have found in ancient garbage is a pod corn. That pod corn is not around anymore. Each kernel of pod corn had its

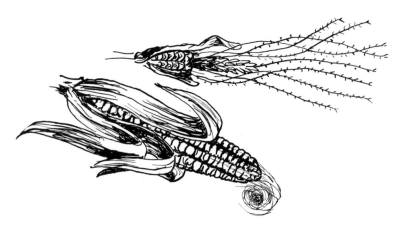

Ancient pod corn and modern corn

own husk, in the normal fashion for nuts and seeds. When the kernels dropped onto the ground, each one had a chance of producing a plant. After the Tehuacanos and other early corn growers cultivated the wild pods, they developed a corn with a cob. That is, they selected kernels that had a tendency to grow together. In time, they had produced a corn that had cobs, with all the kernels under one tough husk. If the cobs fell to the ground, the kernels were trapped inside the husk. This cultivated corn still cross-pollinated easily with wild pod corn. It was the wild corn that changed so that it could not reproduce itself either. It became extinct.

A Tehuacano examining a stalk of pod corn

After the Tehuacanos had cultivated corn they added other crops. Beans and squash were the most important. They became the agricultural trio that supported the great Amerind civilizations of the succeeding eras.

The change from foraging was very gradual everywhere in the Americas. Once the kernel had been planted in the Old World, man gave himself up to the plow completely. Not in the Western Hemisphere. There was a certain freedom that the Amerind was reluctant to abandon.

The people on the Peruvian coast, in the Lomaseros' foraging ground, began their farming in a different way.

In early Archaic times there was still good hunting in the highlands, and there were ready-made crops on the fog meadows and fish in the sea. As the lomas shrank under the altithermal sun, the people depended more and more on fish. By the middle of the fourth millennium B.C. (3500 B.C.), the lomas couldn't support the foraging population.

One group of people took up farming. The crop was squash. These were the Squash people of Encanto and Pampa. The banks of the Chillon River were the only places where the squashes would grow, so that is where they had their gardens.

There were signs that this early attempt at farming suffered a gradual decline. By 2500 B.C. the people had returned to dependence on the sea. The settled time had not been one of total concentration on farming. New foraging tools had been perfected. The Squash people returned to the life on the shore with shell hooks and fishlines made out of plant fibers. They had developed very efficient stone sinkers and gourd floats.

Other coastal Peruvians tried the settled life. There are remains of stone and adobe houses south of the territory of the Squash people. Some are dated even earlier, about 3750 B.C. These people developed a high standard of living for Archaic times. They wore clothing of plant fiber and leather. They had inland gardens and fishnets in the sea.

They played wooden flutes and had cemeteries.

Many crops were introduced into Peru during Archaic times. Lima beans, white potatoes, yams, cotton, and finally corn were grown.

The countries of the Pacific rim affected South Amer-

Archaic coastal Peruvian foragers

ica as well as North America during Archaic times. New World pottery-making seems to have begun on the west coast of South America about 3000 B.C., possibly as a result of Japanese trading. A little later, 2875 B.C. there was pottery in Puerto Hormiga, Colombia, another coastal spot. The Japanese pottery of this period is very distinctive, so it is easy to identify it in the Americas. Other Pacific rim peoples traded and may have migrated to the Western Hemisphere, too.

The Amerinds began to make pottery very late in their history compared to the people of the Old World. There really wasn't much need for clay pots when they had such an abundance of natural containers: gourds, shells, horn, and skins and basket materials. European and Asian archaeologists tend to turn their noses up at early Amerind pottery, but American archaeologists feel the same way about Old World basketry. A slow development in either craft can hardly be a sign of backwardness.

The physical appearance of the western coast people in South America, at least, was altered by Pacific rim people who were active on the ocean at this time. High-bridged noses and high cheekbones are characteristic of some of the Asiatic Pacific rim people, and they show up in the faces of coastal Amerinds.

The big Andean glaciers had melted. The forest people of the south, like those of the north, found new opportunities for good foraging. The woodland foragers of Mexico, Guatemala, Venezuela, Colombia, Ecuador, and Bolivia had a rich life in terms of tools and food. The great rivers may have begun to be the highways of the jungle at this time. Dugouts, which may even have been used by Ice Age foragers, became the main transport.

Shellfish gathering was as important as it was in the north. The people were prosperous. There were art and communication.

Plant cultivation spread into the forests of South and Middle America in late Archaic times.

The coast, the forests, and the deserts of South and Middle America were ready to begin their journey toward civilization. It was a trail that was in perfect harmony with its background. The natural resources of each region were strengthened rather than destroyed at the end of the road.

Llamas and alpacas were domesticated by 1000 B.C.

EARLY AMERIND CIVILIZATIONS: 6

South America

It began with the villages.

By 2500 B.C. permanent villages had appeared on the central coast of Peru. They were built by the foragers who had been collecting seeds and catching fish. Beans, squash, guavas, white and sweet potatoes, and peppers were being grown. When the new crops had a poor season, the people could always fall back on seafood. The villagers were true heirs of the Lomaseros. They were never totally dependent on one source of food.

In 2500 B.C. there were three small permanent villages. Two were on the slopes of the foothills. A third, Punte Grande, was on the beach. The life-style in the villages was more advanced than the Squash peoples' life-style in the Archaic period. Cotton production was one of the reasons for it. There was cloth for clothing, bedding, binding, and containers. Cotton cord was used for fishnets. The weaver became as important a craftswoman as the basket maker or potter.

The populations of the villages grew. By 2000 B.C. there was an abundance of labor and a surplus of food. Under such circumstances men have usually achieved something outside the area of mere food-getting. It may be in art, in political expansion, in scientific exploration, or in social experiments.

With the Peruvians it was religion.

The people on the coast had always paid attention to the usual gods of sea and sky and mountains. By 1800 B.C. they began to show an unusual concentration on religion. A big ceremonial center was built at Chuquitanta, in the Chillon Valley. It had a sanctuary for a god we haven't identified. It had many buildings whose purpose we don't understand. They were surrounded by high stone walls to protect the whole temple complex from some enemy we don't know about. Only the marks of foundations and some crumbling walls are left at Chuquitanta. There is good farmland there. All traces of the happenings at the temple have vanished under a hundred generations of plows.

The villagers planted more corn. They raised peanuts. Llamas, alpacas, and guinea pigs were domesticated, all with the approval of the god of Chuquitanta. Except for turkeys and a few birds that were kept for feathers, these were the only animals that were ever domesticated in the Americas. Dogs, of course, had always been part of the scene. Dogs may have accompanied the scroungers from Asia and mixed with native American dogs.

About 1500 B.C. village unions were formed. Like the earlier isolated villages, they were based on farming and fishing.

Their unity came from belief in the jaguar god.

By that time, the unions had become an economic necessity. Peru had a peculiar geography, even discounting the deserts right by the ocean. The high Andes are immediately behind the deserts. They are cut by narrow valleys that run down to the sea. There is good soil in the flood plains in the lower valleys. They can be farmed if they are irrigated. There is rarely enough

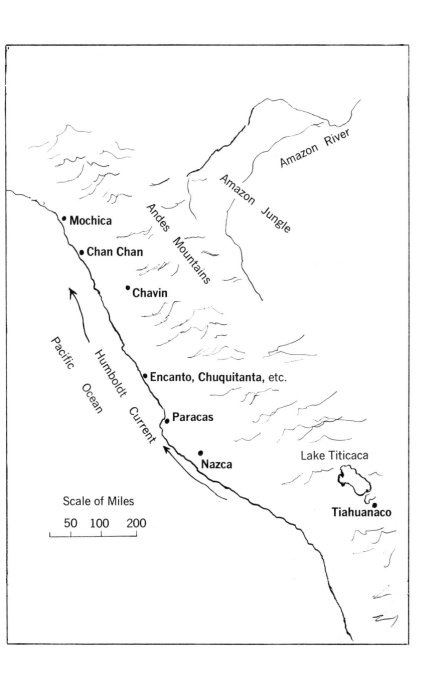

Mochica

Chan Chan

Chavin

Andes Mountains

Amazon River

Amazon Jungle

Pacific Ocean

Humboldt Current

Encanto, Chuquitanta, etc.

Paracas

Nazca

Lake Titicaca

Tiahuanaco

Scale of Miles

50 100 200

An early Peruvian coastal village

water. The water table is very low at the edges of the flood plains. Individual wells can never supply enough irrigation water. The water has to come from the highlands of the valleys, and it has to run their full lengths to get to the flood plains.

Irrigation systems that run the length of a valley require the cooperation of all the villagers of the valley. It was natural that the villages would unite for that purpose. The need for the union came from the necessity for water. The cement was religion. The god was the jaguar.

When the irrigation planners went into the highlands to find the source of the water—the home of the gods, certainly—they came into contact with the mountain people. These people knew both sides of the Andes, the deserts on the west and the Amazon jungle on the east. The god of the jungle wasn't hard to find.

He was the jaguar, both terrible and beautiful to look at. Jaguars are not considered much of a danger today. They are anxious to keep as far away from people as they can. In times when they were more numerous and men were poorly equipped to fight them, they must have aroused feelings of great awe. It isn't surprising that people of both valleys and mountains took up the praise of the cat god. From that time on, the South American liked feline deities and temples that were up high, near the home of the water.

Valleys on both sides of the mountains were producing corn and prospering by 1000 B.C. The people lived on irrigated land, wove cotton cloth, and made fired pottery. These centers gave rise to the first civilizations of Peru.

The earliest was Chavín.

Independent villages in the Chavín Valley developed a mania for the jaguar. There was a mysterious thrill about this religion in the valley. One village chief after another became converted. Some towns became ceremonial centers. The largest was Chavín de Huántar. It was a site high on an eastern slope of the mountains. Its temple was a complex of rooms and galleries that covered two 250 square feet. A stone statue of a man-jaguar stood in an inner sanctum of the temple.

Travel between the city centers became possible and profitable.

Craftsmen in weaving, ceramics, and toolmaking and merchants of religious goods traveled from one ceremonial center to another. They met at the temples to obtain the god's blessing.

The Chavín priests may have spread the cult themselves, or there may have been other missionaries. Their power seems to have been mainly religious. There was

Traveling peddler in Chavín times

no political control of the allied cities. There was no common law that we know about. Chavín de Huántar and the jaguar ruled a religious family of smaller ceremonial center priests and their congregations.

There was a unified art style, too. Pottery with cat faces was one of the Chavín hallmarks. Tabular jug handles that were also spouts were characteristic of many pots. The art style spread to many valleys. Chavín building styles, especially in temples, were similar among the villages of the union.

The union was so strong that even after it ended, about 500 B.C., there was a strong tradition of solidarity. One after another, cultures appeared on the coast. Each built a union along Chavín lines.

The first city to become a center of Peruvian civilization after Chavín de Huánter was Paracas. Paracas was a barren desert peninsula on the southern coast. The Paracasos irrigated extensively. They raised cotton. They kept vicuñas and alpacas and had an advanced textile industry. Their textiles told the stories of their nature myths and their close observation of desert and sea life.

The looms of Paracas gave the world some of the finest cotton and vicuña cloth that has ever been made. It

A Paracas weaver

wasn't only that the Paracasos could weave. How they could embroider! Tiny fish, birds, and animal gods were drawn with almost microscopic stitches.

Paracas unified a small territory around the city and then, about A.D. 400, its culture declined. It was not destroyed. It was incorporated into the Nazca state which was expanding from the south.

Nazca had roots deep in coast foraging traditions. For a long time it was a village of little adobe houses. Even after it became an important center, it could boast only a few flat-topped pyramids and a moderately influential priesthood. Religion was still the unifying force. The hills of Nazca were terraced for farming, which was reasonably successful. There was a little gold and no silver. The Nazca textiles were fair products of the weaver's art, but they were no match for those of Paracas.

The Nazcas seemed to have had little knack for administration.

They had a pottery that has no rival in the Americas.

Collectors and native procurers are so eager for this pottery that they have destroyed many of the old Nazca sites looking for it. Tombs were broken into and mummies were thrown out. Ancient workshops and tools were broken up and scattered in the quest.

Nazca pottery was polished. It was painted. There were as many as eleven colors on some pieces. Blues, purples, and reds that none of the South Americans had ever tried to make before were brushed onto bowls, cups, jugs, jars, and masks. Some of the designs show people. Some are of flowers and animals around Nazca. Some are realistic and some are stylized.

The Nazcas built a loose confederation of cities on the southern coast. For hundreds of years they ruled it independently. Even when the later Tiahuanacan and Inca civilizations spread over the territory, Nazca remained an important center.

In the north, at the same time that the Nazcas were

Nazca craftsman making sculptured pottery

forming and holding together a union of cities, the Mochica civilization flourished.

The land of the Mochicas looks even more forbidding than the desert coast of the south. The rocky, shell-covered beach ends in dunes of gray sand. Beyond the sands are hot, barren foothills and craggy mountains. The sun beats down all day in the spring and summer, and there is no rain. There are only small animals such as lizards and foxes on this desert. The lizards eat the insects that breed in the damp coves along the shore. The foxes eat the blackberries that grow on scrub bushes in the sand. It is hard to see any other movement inland during the day.

Offshore, it's a different story.

The Humboldt current carries its life with it. On the Mochica coast particularly, fish and plankton attract millions of seabirds. Their roosting places are on nearby islands. There are so many kinds and numbers of these birds that they can cover even the blinding summer sun and blacken the yellow Peruvian sky. The birds create one of the richest fertilizers in the world in their breeding grounds on the offshore islands. It is made of their feathers, their droppings, and the remains of their fish kills.

Mochica chiefs claimed descent from a mythical king, Nymlap, who came from the south with a fleet of balsa rafts. The chief, who was also a high priest, had a court and carried a green stone idol that became the Mochica national god.

Even if the Nymlap legend is true, these immigrants were not the first people in the area. Archaic coastal foragers lived near Huaca Prieta in the Chicama Valley as early as 3000 B.C. They lived in adobe houses that were built partly underground. They had taken up farming and raised squash, beans, corn, peppers, yuca, potatoes, and cotton.

The Mochicas, whether they were immigrants or just another local farming group, developed the coastal desert. They built irrigation ditches from the mountains, made terraces on the hills, built weaving workshops, and most important, hauled guano fertilizer from the bird islands offshore.

The fertilizer gave the Mochicas a way to rejuvenate the land constantly. At least three cultures that span the length of the period of Amerind civilizations were made possible by this system of land improvement. They are the Mochica, the Chimu, and the Inca-Chimu. The Huaca Prietas might even have used it. Once the results of fertilizing were seen, llama and human fertilizer were also used. This must have caused bacterial problems, but the practice remained common. The deciding factor in this north country coast area, in its long history of power, was not military strength, compelling religious rites, better administration, or individual genius, but—fertilizer!

The Mochica chiefs seem to have claimed ownership of all the land, llama herds, and workshops. The people had only the right of use, not ownership. The right of use extended to every man, though. When a man married, he had claim to a certain amount of land for cultivation. There were two main classes of people: the workers, who were the producers, and an aristocracy composed of priests, chiefs, royal messengers, soldiers, and royal craftsmen. This second group was totally supported by the working farmer-fishers.

Soldiers in the Mochica state were a long way from

the rough spearmen who had guarded the lands of the earlier city chiefs. They had maces as well as spears and shields. They were uniformed and helmeted according to crops. They were efficient and vigorous campaigners who spread Mochica control over many valleys on the coast. When they were at home, they lived in barracks. Like many modern soldiers, they liked pretty girls and beer.

What we know about the Mochica soldiers, and about many things in everyday day of the Mochicas, we have learned from their pottery. The pottery paintings served as a kind of record book for all their doings. Evidently they did a great deal. The Mochicas seem to have been boisterous and positively hyperactive. Their chief glories were war and pottery, a kind of military-ceramic complex that had great endurance.

The Mochicas were close observers of nature. Owls, monkeys, and deer are woven carefully into textiles. Everyday pottery was often in the shape of animals.

The Mochicas did not neglect their gods. They built many-storied temples to the sun and moon. The chief was the high priest, and even minor chiefs could demand religious tribute. There were trade routes. They led from one temple to another, as they had in Peru since Chavín times. The Mochicas built many more roads than other Peruvians had built. There were at least three main trade routes up and down the coast and into the mountains. Merchants carried religious goods and simple trade wares. They also carried items of great value, like the products of the goldsmith's art.

By A.D. 650 most of the early Andean civilizations were beginning to wane. Even the vigorous Mochicas had a period of decline. The jaguar was only a memory. Temples were falling into disrepair in the south. Burials of important people were more casual. The villages continued to exist, and farmers went on farming. The chiefs probably made new attempts at religious unions centered in their individual cities.

After the Mochica conquests, nothing in the way of a strong union was achieved until the end of the seventh century A.D. Then everything gave way before a new power, the weeping god of the Lake Titicaca country.

Style of Nazca pottery

Mochica owl jug

Mochica gold work: a figure bottle

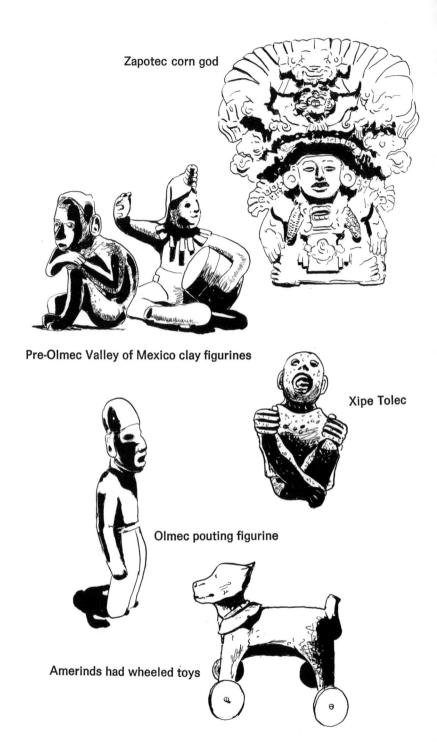

Zapotec corn god

Pre-Olmec Valley of Mexico clay figurines

Xipe Tolec

Olmec pouting figurine

Amerinds had wheeled toys

EARLY AMERIND CIVILIZATIONS:

Middle America

The humid jungle of Central America was the cradle of another very early civilization. It was the home of the Olmec tribes. Many scientists believe that the Olmec civilization was the first true civilization in the Americas.

The Olmec homeland was the state of Veracruz, on the Gulf Coast of Mexico. It is hot and swampy. Tall trees, as high as 160 feet, form a solid canopy of green with their branches. A day without rain is rare. The air is full of mosquitoes. Red and green parrots and macaws dart from one tree to another. Howler monkeys race along the highest branches. Sloths hang from branches below them. Coatimundis inspect the tree trunks for insects. Anteaters, boa constrictors, armadillos, turtles, toads, and tapirs forage among the thick-leafed plants and orchid blossoms on the jungle floor. Jaguars stalk behind huge sprays of fern.

By 1000 B.C. the Olmecs, who were the human foragers in the sweltering place, had come from gathering food to seed cultivation to villages. The villages were religious centers.

The religion was the cult of the jaguar.

The earliest large Olmec ceremonial center that has been found is on the swamp island of La Venta. The

Olmecs who lived around La Venta had to clear the land for their crops and their living quarters. The jungle is particularly thick around La Venta. The big trees had to be felled with stone axes and fire. It was a constant chore to keep the jungle from reclaiming the land. There was plenty of heat and moisture for the corn, but the Olmecs certainly spent as much time on their land, clearing and weeding, as the Peruvians did on their irrigation ditches. Such farming is called "slash and burn."

The Olmecs put a lot of effort into their religion, too. At the site of La Venta they built a great temple and many stone monuments to their gods. Many of these were in the form of huge stone faces. The stone for the monuments had to be hauled for many miles. It had to be carved and placed to suit the priests. The stone masks did not represent kindly gods by any means. Some of them look like angry, pouting babies; others are growling jaguar-men; all are somber.

The Olmecs had a well-developed mosaic art a thousand years before Christ. Squared, colored blocks were laid out at the temple centers. When the entire mosaic was finished, it was covered with clay and left underground. It must have been a special tribute to the gods, giving them an art work without using it at all. The mosaic artists didn't even have the satisfaction of having their work viewed by fellow men.

The priests must have had a powerful influence over the people to get them to build temples and mounds and haul stone. The priests themselves had to be supported by the labor of the Olmec farmers. The prophecies and the fearful aspect of the Olmec religion were the main weapons they used to keep the population working for them.

Olmec farmers supported temples with corn offerings

Why did the hard-working corn planter of Central America obey the priests?

The need for unity in Peru had been the problems involved in irrigating. Nothing like that was needed in the early Olmec lands. So, even with religious fear to account for some of the labor, why were the people willing to support the temple establishment? One answer is that probably not all of them did. The prophecies and ceremonies that excited or frightened many Olmecs must have been nothing more than a burden to others. They apparently didn't revolt. The jungle and the old foraging life were always just a few miles away. Rogue individuals or groups could always return to the forest.

The priests were not military leaders. If there were soldiers at the temples, they served as guards or police. The people around La Venta supported their priests for four centuries because they were willing to do so. They may only have been willing because they were afraid of the priests' mystical power, for it does not seem to have been accomplished by force of arms in those early days.

Olmec priests had great power

The La Venta Olmecs set up or influenced the found-
ing of other ceremonial centers. By 500 B.C. Monte
Albán, in the dry hill country to the north, was a city of
priests and sanctuaries to the gods. The Monte Albán
Amerinds, who were probably ancient Zapotecs, built a
great temple to honor the gods, and they built smaller
houses for the comfort of the priests.

At Monte Albán the people carved big, flat stone
faces in the Olmec style. They developed the Olmec
glyphs, word pictures, into a simple written language.
It was the first written language in the Americas. The
artists painted pictures and put words near the mouths
of their figures. The Monte Albáns were, therefore, the
first American cartoonists.

The site of Monte Albán was different from that of
La Venta. The temple city was high and dry. It stood on
a mountain guarding three cultivated valleys. The
Monte Albáns lived in the valleys, not near the temple.
They met at the temple to exchange ideas, to pay
respect to the gods, and probably to do some trading.

Corn was the main crop below Monte Albán. It was
grown by irrigation. The people carved stone images
of their corn god and worshiped him along with the
Olmec jaguar. Some of the strong, dramatic art styles
that have made Mexican art imitated all over the world
first appeared in some of these religious representations.

Olmec civilization spread north and south. It came
into the Valley of Mexico, where the people had been
cultivating corn and leading settled lives for more than
four thousand years.

The Mexican farmers of the valley seem to have
been more fun-loving and less grim than the Olmecs.
They had a simple religion. It may have had something

to do with the little clay figures that have been found all over that part of Middle America. These figures are doll-like. There are girls and farmers and musicians, all in easy poses, all with contented expressions.

The jaguar was a powerful god. The little clay figures disappeared when his religion invaded the valley.

The mark of Olmec civilization was the ceremonial center. The first one in the Valley of Mexico was the Pyramid of Cuicuilco. It was started about 300 B.C. For many centuries the Mexican farmers trudged to the pyramid with their offerings. It was the center of their world until about A.D. 300.

By that time, Teotihuacán had taken over the leadership of the entire Olmec world.

Teotihuacán was the first real city in the Americas. It was not only a temple center. There were temples to the gods, whole complexes of them, but there were also residential districts.

Important people lived in fine houses inside the city. Some were priests. Others were merchants or land-owners. There were too many houses to make one think that they were just for temple officials.

There were pyramids and temples for the gods. Elaborate rituals were held on ceremonial days. Minor temple functions went on daily.

Parts of Teotihuacán were designed as marketplaces. Trading didn't have to wait for festival days but could go on anytime.

Teotihuacán had carefully laid-out streets. The most important one was called the Street of the Dead. It ran through the downtown section of the city. For about four hundred years marchers in thousands of processionals trod the stone roadbed of the Street of the Dead. Other people, probably hundreds of thousands, who had their minds more on baskets, jugs, corn, and peppers than on ceremonies, walked the same route.

Scientists have estimated that Teotihuacán had a population of 50,000 people when it was at its height. The food needed to feed that many people had to come from the area right around the city.

The Amerinds did not have any wagons or carts; they did not use wheeled vehicles at all. They did know about the wheel, however, for some of their toys had wheels. But they did not have any draft animals; there were no horses, oxen, or donkeys as in the Old World. Llamas and alpacas are not strong enough for the job of pulling heavy wheeled vehicles. At any rate, they were never used in that capacity.

The relation between man and other animals in the Americas was very different from what it was in Asia and Europe. By 10,000 B.C. man had become the dominant animal in the Western Hemisphere. He never thought of himself as the *only* important species.

Farming methods around Teotihuacán improved as the population grew. The old method of abandoning a field after the soil was worn out was changed. Marsh lands were used, and old land was made fertile with marsh muck. Or it was allowed to lie fallow for a few seasons and then used again. Irrigation was extended so that all the dry land could be used. We are not sure just what farming methods were worked out by the farmers in the area. Whatever they were, they kept Teotihuacán booming.

By A.D. 400 the old Olmec gods that had created an empire were minor deities or had disappeared altogether. Teotihuacán had its own gods. They were led by Quetzelcoatl, the feathered serpent, who was probably an iguana originally. Tlaloc, the god of rain, was

Amerinds carried produce on their backs

another important figure. There were some fierce gods, too. At least one of them, Xipe Tolec, demanded human sacrifices. So the priests told the people. On the whole, the gods were understanding and generous, according to the Teotihuacanos.

Teotihuacán had a calendar, a written language, and a number system. The calendar was based on fifty-two years. Every fifty-two years a new calendar was started. Pyramids were rebuilt or enlarged every fifty-two years. Because a new calendar was started at the end of these ceremonial periods, it must have been very difficult for even the ancient Mexicans to keep track of early events. It would have been hard to remember in which fifty-two-year time period an important thing had happened. It is practically impossible now. Even when ancient Mexican writings are uncovered, the events that are described cannot be dated.

Teotihuacán had very good stonemasons and stone carvers. Of all the great cities in Middle America, it has the largest amount and the most skillfully worked examples of stonecraft. Craftsmen of Teotihuacán also painted, stuccoed, wove, and made pottery that was imitated all over Middle America and beyond.

The civilization of the Teotihuacanos spread south into the older Olmec centers and northward into country where the jaguar people had never been. Regions where the semiforaging life had hung on after the introduction of corn planting now turned to full-time farming. Irrigation came into places like the Tehuacán Valley. The people finally abandoned their old round of cactus harvesting and deer hunting under the influence of the civilized Teotihuacanos.

The Teotihuacanos entered the land of the Maya tribes in southern Mexico. But they were not the first to do so.

When Olmec civilization was spreading, about 500 B.C., it pushed into the Petén jungle of northern Guatemala, where Maya woodland foragers were living. The Olmec missionaries or settlers soon had the Mayas clearing land to build a temple. From the start, the Maya plan was to build a maze of small temple centers and farm settlements in the jungle.

The small temples were not living places, not cities at all. They had a pyramid and a temple or two. Their main purpose was to provide a place where the people could bring their offerings on appropriate days and not have to travel too far to do it. The priests in these small centers weren't very important. Some archaeologists even think that they were part-time farmers who changed hats on ceremonial days.

The land around the base of the pyramid served as a marketplace. People could bring their vegetables, their pottery, and their cloth to trade. The Mayas were good farmers, good potters, and good weavers.

The farmers lived in thatched huts beyond the ceremonial areas, with fields laid out behind their houses.

Trails connected the small ceremonial centers. Some followed rivers; others pushed right through the jungle. The trails became roads near the large ceremonial centers. These were not places of occasional worship with part-time priests. From 300 B.C. to A.D. 900, the time of the Old Maya Empire, the great temples controlled the lives of hundreds of thousands of Central American people. The ruins of many of the old Maya temples are still standing. The one at Tikal was one that was well preserved when scientists found it.

The Mayan high priests of the great temple centers developed the Olmec glyph writing into a written language that could be used to transact business, record

Temple at Tikal

history, or describe ceremonial procedures. Some of the writing that has been preserved has been translated. Most has not, however. One of the reasons is that the writing we have is mostly from stonework and is hard to decipher even if the language is understood.

The Mayas did not keep their records on stone, as a rule, but on bark paper. Almost all of these written records were crushed under the Spanish boot heel in the sixteenth-century conquests. The writings were considered to be barbarous and wicked. Bonfires were made of Maya books. Temples were reduced to rubble when they were found. There was a great effort on the part of the earliest Europeans in the New World to obliterate one of its richest civilizations.

The Mayas had developed their writing before 100 B.C. They had also hit upon the idea of using a zero in their number system.

The tally-stick approach to numbers is to treat them as a collection of ones. Using a zero to mean "no quantity" let the Mayas deal with numbers that were longer than any tally stick they could have found. These large numbers could be written by having different places in a number represent different values. No Egyptian ever thought of it. Neither did a Greek or Roman. In India, merchants were using a dot for zero about the time of Christ. Europeans didn't know about it until after A.D. 700 when the India-Persia-Arabia caravan route was established. The Mayas had been using zero for hundreds of years by that time.

Between 400 B.C. and 200 B.C. the high priests created a calendar. Mayan astronomers had found out that the year is a little more than 365¼ days long. The calendar was built on this. It may have been the greatest intellectual accomplishment of all the Amerinds. It was more accurate than any calendar used in any part of the world until the seventeenth century.

All this knowledge gave the members of the high-priest class enormous power. They could interpret the pleasure of the wrath of the gods. They could measure time by signs and pictures, and they could compute with numbers, the ultimate data-processing accomplishment. The priests were supported in luxury for doing the tasks connected with appeasing the gods. They had been given leisure to do an organizational job connected with it, interpreting the science of time and the heavens. They did a good job, but they repaid their toiling supporters by keeping the knowledge of the discoveries to themselves.

The Maya number system was based on twenty instead of ten, the way ours is. In Maya writing, a zero, which was written 〈◯〉 meant twenty times a number instead of ten times the number, the way our zero does. A dot • meant one. A long bar ▬ meant five. Numbers could grow rapidly in this system.

• = 1	▬▬ = 10	
▬ = 5	••	•
•• = 7	••••	〈◯〉 = 20
▬	▬▬ = 280	
••••	〈◯〉	
▬▬ = 19		

The priests were judges and tax collectors as well as religious leaders. The haughty Maya priest of the Old Maya Empire had no rival in the New World as far as power went.

There was usually a bustle of activity around the great temple cities. They attracted the best products and the most talented people of the countryside. The most skillful weavers, who worked on the fine, brightly colored ritual costumes, lived near the pyramids. The most beautiful pottery and cloth came to the temple cities. The most accomplished architects and builders worked on the pyramids and the temples, which were always being constructed or repaired. Sons of chiefs who were privileged to have the friendship of the priests were brought to the temple cities, were given the best possible training, and became scientists or priests.

There was drama in the large centers. Some of it has been preserved in the crumbling walls which have been dug out of the jungles. One temple, which has been named Bonampak by modern scientists, tells the story of a raid and a ritual sacrifice that were planned in the temple.

Maya glyphs

There are paintings of priests who are dressed as gods. There are a crab god, a crocodile god, and a snake

Maya chief guards a prisoner

Maya farmers worked hard at their crops

god. Soldiers in splendid uniforms march across the walls. They are no mere temple guards but an elite military unit. Important people listen to the priests giving orders for the raid. They wear jaguar robes, heavy necklaces of jade, and carved bracelets and earrings, and they carry quetzal feathers.

The victims are poor villagers who wear nothing but cotton loincloths. After they are captured, they plead for their lives. They are killed, trumpets sound, gourd rattles are shaken, and drums are beaten. The priests explain that the gods are pleased.

The gods and styles of Teotihuacán had come into Maya country by the time of Bonampak. Perhaps it was these northern gods who had demanded the bloody sacrifices, or perhaps the idea was homegrown in Maya country. Whatever the origin of the custom, it continued to be important all through Central American civilized history.

Perhaps, in the beginning, these bloody acts did not affect the Mayan farmers much. The great body of them continued to make their corn flour, grow their beans, and raise their pretty, honey-colored, sloe-eyed babies. They must have been impressed by the science, the architecture, and the art of the temple people. They probably understood how little the priests needed in the way of intellectual powers to conduct the religious murders. Several thousand years later a philosopher remarked that it takes no great genius to kill one's fellow man. People like the adept Maya farmers would have been thoroughly aware of this.

There were still foragers in the jungles. There were still scroungers on the continent. There were many people who were halfway between that life and farming. In the hill country, north of the Valley of Mexico, some of these less civilized people had developed a liking for raids on their settled neighbors. About 700 A.D. Teotihuacán fell to one of these wild groups, the Chichimecs, the "Sons of the Dog."

The city was looted and put to the torch. The people were killed or driven away. In Maya country the temples held out for more than a century after this. Then they too were overrun and the sites abandoned. The Mayas trekked to the peninsula of Yucatán to start a new empire.

Hohokam pottery and
carved stone horned toad

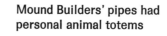

Yucca fiber bag

Mound Builders' pipes had
personal animal totems

Adena stone art

EARLY AMERIND CIVILIZATIONS:

8

North America

The Sons of the Dog were not the only tribe in the dry country north of the Valley of Mexico. Many other desert foragers and farmers lived there. These north Mexican people did not have a high standard of living themselves. They form what has been called a Culture Bridge, connecting the civilizations of the south with the territory that is now the United States.

The Culture Bridge was most important from 1500 B.C. to 500 B.C., where many important ideas about planting, pottery making, and building moved north across the bridge from Mexico. Some ideas from the north, particularly from the deserts, moved south, too. Some scientists believe that the Gulf of Mexico should be considered part of the Culture Bridge.

During the Culture Bridge era, corn growing spread as far as the eastern seaboard of the present United States. From that time until the coming of the Europeans corn was the main subsistence crop of the Americas. The corn belt that ran from Guatemala in the south to the Ohio Valley and Atlantic coast in the north fed a population that ran into millions. If the Fertile Crescent of the Near East was the Bread Basket of the Old World, then this corn belt was the Tortilla Basket of the New. Some of the people who ate from it were highly civilized; others were lowly farmer-foragers. Most of them raised, besides corn, the other two crops in the trio, beans and squash.

The Hohokam (the "Vanished Ones") of central and southern Arizona were one of the more advanced Tortilla Basket peoples. They were descendants of the desert seed gatherers who had been so close to developing agriculture in Archaic times. By 1500 B.C. they had begun cultivating corn. They settled down into communities of little pit houses that were roofed over with mesquite branches. Ground-level huts would not have kept them nearly as cool as the pits.

By 100 B.C. the Hohokam were making pottery. The method of pottery making was borrowed from the south, but the designs were original. Most of the pottery was red or the color referred to in the fashion magazines today as desert tan. Crisscross lines, curls, and tiny animals and people ran around the sides of the bowls and jars. The Hohokam also made ornamental vessels of shell. Some of these shells have designs etched with acid.

The Hohokam settled near the Gila and Salt rivers. They built dams on these rivers and used the water to irrigate their crops. The faint lines of their canals and ditches can still be traced along the hard Arizona ground.

The biggest town the Hohokam built was one that modern Arizonans call Snaketown. Snaketown was not a ceremonial city run by arrogant priests or the preserve of a petty soldier chief; it was a farmers' town of cool little houses and storage buildings.

The Hohokam built some structures that may have been pyramids, whose foundations have been found. Perhaps they were used as centers for astronomical observation, for we know that the Hohokam studied the stars and used a kind of astronomy in their planting. Knowledge of star positions and the science of astronomy were one of the early borrowings from Mexico.

The connection between the Hohokam and Middle America remained strong. The Hohokam even borrowed a Mayan ball game. Remains of the ancient court and one of the rubber balls have been found at a Hohokam site.

Between A.D. 500 and 800, which was an expansive time in the whole Tortilla Basket, the Hohokam culture spread in Arizona. The people occupied sites near riverbeds. At these places there was a good opportunity for them to put their engineering and irrigation methods to work. They came into direct and, apparently, peaceful contact with another desert group. They had known of these people before and had helped pass along southern ideas, including farming, to them. They were the Anasazi, the "Old People," who lived north and east of Hohokam territory.

The Anasazi were one of the Tortilla Basket people who were somewhat less intense about their farming at this time. They had had knowledge of corn cultivation by 100 B.C., but they were more reluctant to give up their caves. They still used the caves for storage after they began to live in the open near their fields.

Many of the things we know about the Anasazi, who are called Basket Makers in their early period, comes from these caves. The name "Basket Makers" was given to them for the obvious reason that this was their chief skill. They wove square-toed sandals, mats, and nets, as well as baskets, out of the fibers of desert plants. They were very careful weavers of straw. This may have been what they contributed to the cultural exchange with other people.

The desert people of northern Arizona had been making baskets for a very long time. Desert Culturists in the Adaptive period, Cochise Seed Gatherers in Archaic times, and finally the Basket Makers of the Tortilla Basket perfected the art. The Anasazi had other arts, too, that may have been involved in trading. They made and smoked cigar-shaped pipes. These pipes may have appealed to any farmer with a heap of corn silk around. A basket would catch the eye of a Hohokam housewife, but the pipe would sell her husband.

The Anasazi grew corn and squash near places like Grand Gulch, Utah, and Four Corners, where Utah, Arizona, Colorado, and New Mexico touch.

The little feathered darts that were used to hunt desert animals much earlier were still around at Anasazi sites. The Basket Makers ate the meat of animals like the rabbit and used the fur for blankets and apron-skirts which they wore in winter. After the altithermal heat wave had run its course, northern Arizona became cooler and much less desertlike in many places.

The Basket Makers gradually gave up their foraging. They irrigated their farms and domesticated wild turkeys. By A.D. 700 their lives were probably just as settled as those of the Hohokam. There was a lot of difference between the towns that the two peoples built. The Hohokam lived in separated houses, either the pit type or the ground-level adobe. The Anasazi seemed to like to live close together in multiple dwellings that were almost on top of one another. New architecture, based on this living feature, was developing at the end of the period.

The move to the cornfields and settled lives bypassed

the Great Plains. The Plains were recovering slowly from the effects of the altithermal drought and were still sparsely settled. There is no evidence that corn growing or irrigation was even attempted at this time. The Great Plains sites that date between 2500 B.C. and A.D. 700 show that the ancient plains foraging pattern was still the prevailing way of life.

There was a new interest in hunting. Antelope and deer bones are more numerous in the rubbish. The modern species of bison was coming onto the plains. Some of them were taken in the course of foraging, though no herd hunting culture appears. Weapon points show this new interest. These points, in several styles, were crude when compared to Clovis and Folsom points, but they seem to have been effective. The toolmakers had been a long time away from concerns with big game.

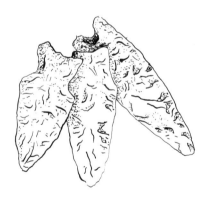

Crude Plains spearpoints
of about 1500 B.C.

The people of Pictograph Cave, Montana, and the Wyoming Basin people are examples of Plains cultures in North America during the time of the Old Maya Empire in Central America and the Mochicas in South

America. The comparison makes the Plains people
seem as primitive as foragers always look when they are
compared to farmers. The Plains tool kit had hunting
weapons, plant-gathering tools, millstones, and simple
baskets. The people used pieces of bone for tally sticks.
Some scientists think that the tally-marked bones in
Pictograph Cave were used to keep score in some kind of
Plains game.

The plainsmen were nomads. They had contact with
the desert people and the woodland people to the east.
A very large part of eastern and western North America
was still plains. Some of the woodland people edged
onto the plains in the east and left unmistakable evidence of their presence during the period of 2500 B.C.
to A.D. 700.

It was the time of the Mound Builders.

The Midwest was still the meeting ground for northern and western ideas. Now southern ideas were added,
coming by the Tortilla Basket route. The descendants
of the Old Copper people were raising corn with the
usual beans and squash and a newer crop, tobacco, early
in the period.

The Mound Builders were the most advanced culture at the northern edge of the Tortilla Basket. They
were the climax of northern centralization. After this
time in Amerind history, the Peruvian unions went on
to become the Inca confederation. The Mayas created a
new empire while the Mexicans united as a warrior
nation and the Anasazi combined to build the Pueblo
culture. In the Midwest it is the earlier period that
represents the high-water mark of unified development.
The Mound Builders were the most civilized society that
the Midwest would know.

The first mounds built by the Mound Builders were

Mound building and the important role of the shamans began with burial rituals

burial places. Important people were buried with some of their possessions and with offerings to the gods. A mound of dirt was placed on top of the grave. Other important people died and were buried on top of the first mound. The mounds rose higher and higher—50, 60, 70 feet into the air. More mounds were built near the first one, and the whole cemetery was enclosed in a thick earthen wall. The inside area was made into a sanctuary for the gods.

The mounds themselves came to have a religious significance. Sometimes they were built alone, not as graves at all. They took many shapes; many were geometric. In the Great Lakes region they were made to look like animals or other natural figures.

The Midwest people who built the mounds were the Adenas and the Hopewells. The Adenas were probably in the area before mound-building days, while the Hopewells probably came from farther east. At one time the Adenas were thought to be the ancestors of the Hopewells, but scientific dating methods have showed this is wrong. The two peoples lived in the Midwest at the same time.

The Hopewells developed faster and had the more advanced culture of the two. They had a strong religion and the kind of data-processing skill that had made the earlier foragers of the area prosperous. The strong religion built the mounds, which the Adenas imitated. The data-processing skill turned the scattered mound centers into a well-fed confederation.

The mounds became temple centers where there were quarters for priests and their assistants. All the trappings that go with conducting rituals were supplied. Courtyards and gardens were designed for the comfort of the priesthood. Living quarters were built inside the walls for them. The area inside the walls of the mounds was something like the plan of a European abbey.

There were no Mound Builder villages. The temples were on high dry ground, and the farms were on the flood plains of the rivers. The people lived in huts near their fields. The more important families among them had the better plots of ground above the flood line, while the poorer people had the lower land. It was fertile, but the huts would be washed out every few years and would have to be rebuilt. The good soil in the Midwest kept both classes content, or at least tied to farming. Scientists who have dug into and around the mounds have found that the more well-to-do among them led very fine lives. They had comfort, security, and wealth in terms of possessions.

In early times the belongings of a herd hunter, a tundran, or a forager could be considered in only one way: how useful they were to the owner. They fit into the life-style as tools. An artifact might be a decorated tool, but it was still a tool. With the Hopewells and Adenas, those rules for discussing possessions don't hold. The only purpose behind some items is pleasure. The high priest could account for his feathered robe for ceremonial reasons, but what about the mantle of a private citizen? Some of them were embroidered with hundreds of mussel pearls. Rich Mound Builders had copper, silver, a little gold, jewelry made of precious stones, pipes with carved figures balanced on them, pendant necklaces, and necklaces of teeth and claws.

One necklace is a chain of tiny bird skulls. A people who could think in terms of massive earthworks also focused on the beautiful lines in something as small as the headbones of a lark.

There were elaborate hats and exotic goods from dis-

Prosperous Hopewell woman and children

tant places. Florida conch shells, shark teeth, Rocky Mountain grizzly bear claws, and Mexican silverware were among their belongings. The display of goods would fill many art museums.

The Hopewells and Adenas liked to fondle a beautiful pipe or wear a soft shirt or decorate themselves with a bracelet, a necklace, or a headdress. They liked to have things that couldn't be worn at all, just to look at.

The Mound Builders liked to possess things for the joy of recognizing a beautiful material and having a beautiful product created from it. Possessiveness, acquisitiveness, greed the Puritans called it. Whatever it was, the Mound Builders built their lives on it. They created, and what they couldn't make they imported.

There were no roads in Hopewell-Adena country, such as there were in Central and South America. As far as we know, these peoples did not even have an organized system of footpaths as the Maya did. The rivers were the highways. They were the means for the best transportation system in the Americas. Since the Amerinds never used wheels, waterways were the best routes for hauling goods. The canoes of the Midwest were the most efficient vehicles. Canoe material was available in large quantities. The people learned how to use fire, framing forms and ribbing to make both dugouts and the lighter variety of canoe. They continued this craft even after their golden days were over.

Some mound-building projects were on fortified hills. Every state east of the Mississippi has the remains of such forts. They have one or two thick walls of earth or stone. Inside the walls, there was an area big enough to house the defenders of the hill and shelter people who came there for protection. Some forts had artificial reservoirs to store water in the event of a siege.

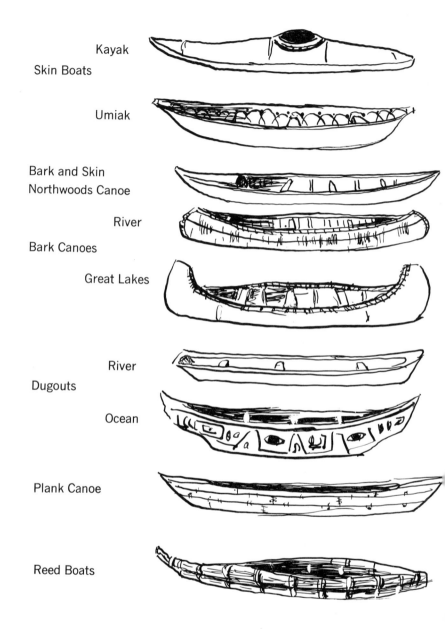

Kayak

Skin Boats

Umiak

Bark and Skin
Northwoods Canoe

River

Bark Canoes

Great Lakes

River

Dugouts

Ocean

Plank Canoe

Reed Boats

Main types of Amerind watercraft

Who was the enemy?

For the Hopewells, it was probably the Adenas. The Hopewells were wealthier and more settled and had more to protect than the Adenas. The Adenas were probably the older, more barbaric population that raided the fat Mound Builder centers of the Hopewells when they could. They built their own mounds, too, just as the Germanic tribes had their own fortified villages outside the Roman imperial walls. The Adenas produced less and their goods were inferior. They were probably part-time hunters and foragers. They would have been a lot tougher than the Hopewells.

The Adenas and Hopewells lived near the same rivers. They used the same kind of materials, including copper, and grew the same kinds of crops. They probably stole one another's women for brides.

About A.D. 800 something happened to the Hopewell-Adena Mound Builders, especially to the Hopewell element. They stopped trading with distant people and stopped building. Their tools and wares became poor and downright primitive. What happened? It may have been disease, rebellion, or war between the two groups of Mound Builders. The woods were full of insects that carry diseases, so a plague, something like malaria, is possible. The great earthworks required more labor than some of the Egyptian pyramids. Maybe the people who had always done the backbreaking work took a long look at what they were getting out of it. Perhaps there was a reversal in the good weather that the Midwest had enjoyed during this time. The people may have been forced to put more time in on their crops. It may have been a matter of feuding between important families. It may have been a full-scale war in which

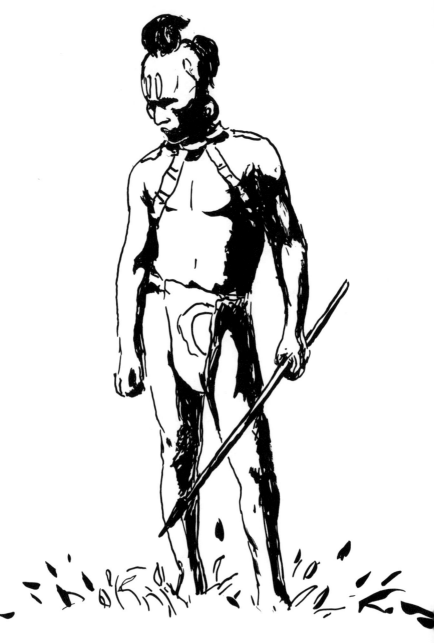

A Hopewell warrior

the Hopewells and Adenas almost swallowed each other.

Whatever the reason, the two cultures were reduced to a level where they were not distinguishable from each other or from the foraging people near them. The society of Mound Builders on their river highways broke into many smaller cultures and then into scattered tribes.

Tiahuanacan urn

Chimu gold sacrificial knife

Inca luxuries: gold staff head,
agate alpaca, gold lime spoon

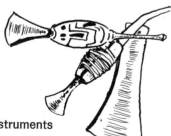

Inca bronze surgical instruments

IMPERIALISM AND DIVERSITY: 9

The Andean Empires

In A.D. 700 the people of the Andes came under the spell of a new religion. The god lived at Tiahuanaco, in the Aymaras' country. He was a stiff, two-headed cougar god who cried great carved tears over some tragedy that has been forgotten. The tears made the rains in the mountains and filled the irrigation ditches below.

Tiahuanaco was on the southern end of Lake Titicaca, which now forms part of the border between Peru and Bolivia. It is very high, more than 12,000 feet above sea level. The country around the lake is brown and barren. It makes the icy, gleaming waters of the big lake stand out even more sharply than if the mountains were wooded, and the lake's surface reflects higher snow-covered peaks.

Lake Titicaca was the cradle of legends in the Andes. Even before the weeping god, it was regarded with awe. The holy of holies was an island in the center of the lake. The sun and moon themselves were said to have come out of a red sandstone cave on the island.

Lake Titicaca was on the highland route from the north. Scroungers coming south before the Adaptive period may have been the first inhabitants, the original ancestors of the Aymaras.

Boats on Lake Titicaca

The temple of Tiahuanaco was built with huge blocks of stone. They were hauled, squared, and laid by men who must have had tremendous endurance. The thin air of the high Andes makes ordinary men tired after even a short walk. Wonderful stonework became the hallmark of the Tiahuanacan empire. Stones were laid without mortar. They were fitted together so skillfully that archaeologists have noticed a knife blade cannot be slipped between them.

It was so cold and high near Lake Titicaca that the people couldn't raise much food. Most of them lived far down the mountain where there was enough warmth and fertile soil to grow crops. In this way they were able to support a growing population.

The Tiahuanacanos spread the worship of their god into the valleys along the Pacific coast of South America. They went inland too, toward the jungle, and brought back the old unity that the Chavín jaguar had created many centuries before.

The Tiahuanacanos must have been good soldiers, although they didn't have any better weapons or organization than other Andean people. They were not as wealthy as most of their neighbors. They appear to have been unrelated to them by blood, so the union

Tiahuanacan stone masonry

was not a natural family confederation. The reason for Tiahuanacan success has to be attributed to the missionary work of the temple cultists.

The Andean people, particularly the Peruvians and the Bolivians, became excited by certain kinds of religious ideas. The god who lived at Tiahuanaco was high enough to be in contact with the heavens, or at least the rain clouds. He took the form of a cougar, an animal of the forest, mountain, and valley. He could be revered by diverse peoples for these qualities. Besides, there is a lot to be said for a god who knows how to cry.

Under the leadership of Tiahuanaco, cities were rebuilt and roads repaired. The Tiahuanacan chiefs had military garrisons stationed along the roads from Ecuador to central Chile and into the mountains. These kept order and protected travelers. From A.D. 700 to 1000, they were unchallenged in the central Andean region.

The Tiahuanacanos developed metallurgy and spread the industry throughout their empire. They found the native copper in a different state than had the Old Copper people of Archaic North America. Unlike the Great Lakes copper, Andean copper had to be smelted. The rock ore had to be processed to produce pure copper. The Tiahuanacanos soon had several copper alloys, including bronze. Perhaps the weapons used in keeping the peace were also bronze in later Tiahuanacan times.

The Chavíns had brought social unity through religion. The Tiahuanacanos brought this and more. They achieved the first political union in western South America. Some old cultures were allied and others destroyed. The Nazcas finally lost their identity.

Some people were not so completely absorbed.

The fertilizer kingdom of the Mochicas flirted with the new religion for a while. They may have been associated with Tiahuanaco in some political way, for their art work shows Tiahuanacan influence. In the long run, however, they preferred their own ways and remained outside the empire because they could back up their preferences with arms. The Mochicas were always too active, too independent, too nationalistic, and too militant to form a union with anyone else unless it was under their rule. Even a compelling religion could not change them.

There are traditions that say a new ruling family seized control of the Mochica lands from the descendants of Nymlap. This may have been a palace guard revolt and not a new arrival from outside, as some of the stories say. A new wave of enthusiasm did begin sometime in the ninth century. It was centered at a city-state called Chanchan. The kings called themselves the Chimu.

Chanchan was in the valley of the Moche River, one of those fertile ribbons that threaded down from the mountains through the desert and to the sea. The city was 6 miles square. It was encased in 40-foot-high adobe and stone walls. Chanchan was a victim of urban sprawl, in spite of its careful interior planning. Hundreds of small adobe houses were built helter-skelter outside of the walls.

The inner city was very grand. Three large pyramids provided the focus for religious and social life. Streets were straight and paved. There were parks and gardens. Stone-lined reservoirs held water for the city's needs. It was drawn by irrigation ditches from the Moche River up the valley. Granaries and markets held the produce of the terraced hills behind the city.

The sling, an important Inca weapon

The Chimus decorated many of the walls inside the city with paintings and relief sculptures. Great numbers of artists and craftsmen must have been at work in the city all the time.

The Chimus built roads between the valleys and replaced old Mochica trails with highways. They built up the llama herds for transport. Llama culture reached a high point with the Chimus.

Besides being beasts of burden, llamas were used for meat. It could be dried into a kind of pemmican. Hides made rough sacking wool. The llama was even used for religious purposes. Every interior organ of a dead llama was examined to see if there were any messages from the gods. Modern people may consider it a strange pipeline from heaven, but the Chimus thought very highly of their llamas. Favorite llamas were pampered. All were treated with great care. A vase painting shows llamas wearing fringed sunshades to keep the glare out of their eyes.

After A.D. 1000 there was another period of Andean decline in the south. The highland empire and the coastal towns that had been under Tiahuanacan control show decay. The union broke into smaller and smaller parts. Some of the fragments were inhabited by old, wealthy farming groups with well-established cities. Others were new tribes made up of several peoples of the old empire. Many were so primitive that they had only small villages.

One of the most primitive communities was Cuzco, the Inca center. The Incas were rough country folk, only a few generations out of mountain caves. They thought of themselves in a very special way, however. Inca mythology naturally claimed beginnings in heaven. The Sun sent his children down into a cave in an

Andean hill. The hill was called the Hill of the Three Windows because there were three cave openings in the side.

There were originally four sons and four daughters of the Sun. The wisest son was Manco Capac, and the wisest daughter was Mama Ocllo. The other children conveniently died or were killed when the Inca clans, which also came out of a cave, looked for a new land.

The Incas came to a valley where primitive people lived. These people, according to the story, accepted the Incas' rule. The Incas, who had arrived well versed in agriculture and crafts, taught all the valley people.

At least two tribes were unimpressed. Inca history records bitter fighting between them and the Urubamba and Chancas. One Inca after another worked on proving his divinity to them. The Incas raided, traded, and allied to make a strong little city out of Cuzco, their original village center. They were probably even more primitive than their neighbors when they arrived and learned their farming and crafts from them. They were good fighters, however, until the eighth Inca. He deserted the field of battle with his oldest son when the Chancas were getting the best of him. The day was saved by another son, Inca Pachacuti. Pachacuti won the battle and took the Sun title away from his father.

The year was A.D. 1436. Inca history was about two hundred years old.

Pachuti built the Inca army into hard-hitting, fast-moving units. Llama pack trains kept the army supplied, and relays of runners kept the Inca in constant touch with his capital.

The Inca conducted quick, decisive campaigns against his neighbors. First, he ended any threat to Cuzco, then turned his attention to the eastern Andean valleys. He took over the cities there and led his armies to the edge of the Amazon jungle. Next the northern cities, including Tiahuanaco itself, were taken.

The Incas conquered many cities by military force, but a large number fell to the golden tongues of Inca ambassadors. These men had developed the art of making local chiefs bow to the Inca without having a spear raised. Their message was simple enough: the chiefs had nothing to fear for themselves or their children if they accepted Inca rule. This message was presented with enticing glimpses of the luxurious life of Inca nobles and their allies and the horrible conditions under which rebellious chiefs lived.

The Inca lived up to his ambassadors' promises. He didn't allow pillaging or mistreatment of the people or the chiefs who accepted his rule without battle.

After Pachuti finished his military campaigns, he had an empire. It was a new kind of empire. All the conquered peoples were absorbed into Inca culture. Quechua, the language of Cuzco, became the official trade language. Young people all over the empire were taught to speak it. There were many common laws. Widows and children anywhere in the empire were supported if they had no means of their own. Food was provided when there was a threat of famine in any part of the Inca's realm. Schools in Cuzco enrolled students from many places in the empire. Technical aid for farming and building came from the capital.

The Inca state was heading toward nationalism and socialism.

A plan called the Mitima helped break down old loyalties. The Mitima was a resettlement of tribes that were too independent in their home territory. The people got help when they were moved; builders, irri-

Inca social security: widows and needy children
were supported by the state

gation experts, and seeds came from Cuzco to encourage
a good start in their new homes.

The Incas were the greatest of the Amerind road
builders. One Inca highway ran along the coast, from
one end of the empire to the other. It was the equivalent of a modern road from New York to San Francisco.
Another one climbed the crest of the Andes mountains.

Suspension bridges hung over rivers and gorges.
They were the wonders of the ancient engineer's craft.
Rope cables, sometimes a foot thick, swung from stone
towers on each side of the gorge. Wood planks were

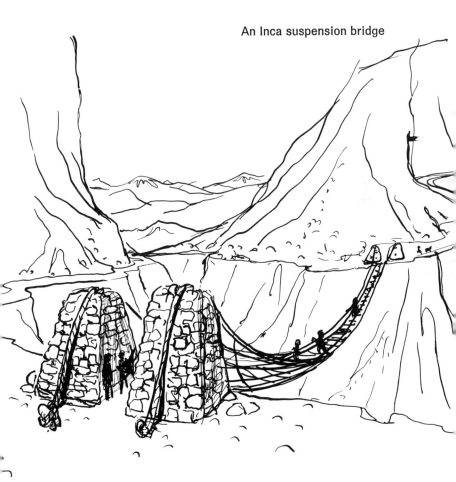

An Inca suspension bridge

laid across the cable to make the roadbed. The suspension bridges swayed and dipped with every step, yet whole armies marched across them.

Some of the suspension bridges which were built in the 1400's were still used in the nineteenth century. There are Inca suspension bridges that are in place today, though the Peruvian government has reinforced them with steel cables.

Many of the roads were paved, and landscaping was provided by the Inca highway department. The roads provided a means of comfortable travel for the people of the empire as well as an expressway for Inca runners. The runners worked in relays between way stations, carrying official parcels and messages. It is generally believed that the Incas had no written language and that all messages would have to be passed by word of mouth. However, there is some new evidence that indicates there may have been glyph writing on the coast and that the Incas could have used it. The writing, if it is that, was invented by the Mochicas. It was painted on large types of lima beans called *pallares*. Lima beans might seem like bizarre stationery to us, but to a desert dweller paper made of wood pulp might seem odd, too.

Eventually, the government at Cuzco controlled the distribution of all goods and most services. The land, the manufacturing shops for dying and weaving wool, and the llama herds were all government-owned. State schools trained scientists. Inca medicine advanced to the stage where Inca doctors could perform brain surgery and pain-killing drugs were used.

The Inca state controlled not only what are regarded as public affairs but also regulated the private lives of the people. A young man had to take a wife before he reached a certain age or he was given one from a lottery. Some regulations made for prosperity. Others must have been hard on the people. They were all cared for, but there were serious limitations on their freedom.

After Pachuti died, his son, Topa Inca, became emperor. He made the empire even larger and Cuzco even richer. The Chimus, who had never listened to the beguiling ambassadors, fell to the Incas. The Inca generals simply cut off the irrigation water to Chanchan and waited until the reservoir ran dry.

The western coast of South America had a golden age. With no wheeled transport vehicles, no advanced number system or national unit of money, and at best a written language of glyphs, the Incas had created one of the New World's great civilizations.

Topa Inca was an enthusiastic explorer. East of the Andes he had an armada of canoes built and took them down one of the Amazon's tributaries toward the great river itself. The hot, insect-infested jungle turned him back before he had reached the mainstream. Still, he had investigated more of the Amazon region than any coast or mountain man before him. Even in modern times only a few men, except for native tribesmen, have explored the Amazon country.

The emperor took a fleet of rafts out into the Pacific Ocean. One group of Inca historians believes that he sailed all the way to the Galapagos Islands more than 600 miles from the Peruvian coast. They have not been inhabited by any known people and support that odd menagerie that helped Darwin organize his ideas about evolution when he visited them four hundred years later. No one can help envisioning the picture of the Inca seeing it as his raft put in. He had seen many

An Inca oceangoing balsa raft

strange sights in the corners of his empire, but never anything like the great tortoise, the seagoing iguanas, and boobies and other birds that had no fear of man.

Topa Inca died in 1493, and his son Huayna Inca became emperor. During his rule a strange sickness swept down from the north and raged through the empire. As many as 10,000,000 people were living in Inca cities at this time. Hordes of them died. In 1525 the plague struck down the emperor. Scientists agree that it was a European disease, probably smallpox.

Statue of Toltec warrior

Quetzalcoatl

Mixtec gold
and turquoise brooch

The Hummingbird god

Aztec god of flowers

IMPERIALISM AND DIVERSITY: *10*

Central American Warrior Kings

The Chichimecs were the "Sons of the Dog" because they were nomadic. The people in the Valley of Mexico did not mean any more than that by the expression. They had probably known the Chichimecs for centuries. To people like the Teotihuacanos the Chichimecs were savage and uncouth, even if they were semisettled corn growers. The tribes of the Chichimecs had no cities or temples or high priests.

But they did have one highly developed specialty— war. The warrior Chichimecs were fierce and mobile. As long as Teotihuacán and the other cities of Central America supported strong armies, kept up their fortifications, and watched the movements of the barbarians, the city people held out. In A.D. 700, for some reason, the defenses were down. Chichimec waves rolled over the Mexican countryside; Teotihuacán and other old pyramid-cities fell; the people were scattered.

From that time on, the gods of Middle America bowed to the war god. The Chichimecs settled on old Olmec lands and intermingled with the earlier people. A few small, crude towns were built, the old builders and the old skills were not available to the barbarians.

There were more invasions from the north. The newer Chichimec warriors found themselves fighting

A Chichimec barbarian

their relatives who had settled down earlier in Mexico. Sometimes the newer raiders were successful; often they were driven away.

The Toltecs were one of these later Chichimec tribes. After A.D. 900 under their chief Mixcoatl they moved into Mexico, where they took over farmlands from other Chichimecs and the ancient Mexican farmers. The Toltecs fitted easily into the old culture. They cultivated the land and learned irrigation and the old crafts from their neighbors. They built a city, Culhuacán, which soon claimed a ring of farming communities. The Toltecs demanded allegiance and, probably, tribute from them. By the time Mixcoatl died, his son, Topiltzin, could call himself a king.

Topiltzin was a successful soldier, but he was also a scholar. He spent a good part of his time contemplating the situation of his own people and the old civilization that the Toltecs had replaced. His favorite god was Quetzalcoatl, the feathered serpent, which had been one of the chief Teotihuacanian gods and represented the old, civilized, gentler ways. Topiltzin even took the name of Quetzalcoatl because he respected the god so much.

Topiltzin built a new city called Tula. It was built by as many of the old artisans as Topiltzin could find and settle near him. About A.D. 970 it became the most important city in Middle America.

Topiltzin began to have serious trouble with his priests and generals when he tried to make Quetzalcoatl the chief god of the city. Many thought that their own violent Chichimec gods were their main strength and did not want to give them up for the doubtful security of a gentle god like Quetzalcoatl. They backed Tezcatlipoca, a god who demanded frequent human sacrifices.

Human sacrifices meant war to obtain victims, and war meant power for the priests of Tezcatlipoca.

Since Topiltzin was a very popular king, the military faction had to figure out a way to get him to abdicate of his own free will. According to Toltec legend, they did it by trickery, by getting Topiltzin drunk enough to disgrace himself.

Topiltzin-Quetzalcoatl left Tula and went to the old Mexican town of Cholula, a stronghold of ancient philosophy and art. After abdicating his title to the Toltec crown, he was so brokenhearted that he could not find happiness even in Cholula. He was last seen taking a boat out into the Pacific. Before he sailed, he promised friends who had come down to the shore with him that he would return at some future time. He gave them a calendar date more than five hundred years in the future. It was 1519. By one of history's most freakish accidents, that was the year of the Spanish arrival in Mexico.

Tula continued to be the leader of Middle America. It was not the same kind of city-state that the Olmecs, the Mayas, and the Teotihuacanos had known, but was more like a modern state. Taxes were set and collected from the countryside in the form of tribute. The authority of the military class was absolute. No one could stand against it after Topiltzin had gone. There were kings who were military leaders and high priests in almost equal proportions.

Toltecs colonized the whole of Mexico from coast to coast and from northern Chichimec desert country to Maya land in the south.

The Maya civilization that had spread to the Yucatán peninsula was thriving. The jungle had claimed the old pyramid centers in Guatemala. In the eleventh century the Toltecs invaded Yucatán and claimed the newer Mayan cities. It was one of those conquests that end with the conqueror getting more like the conquered every day.

The Toltecs absorbed the high culture of the Mayas. They built a new civilization together and constructed

A Toltec Caribbean expedition

the Maya city of Chichén Itzá. The Toltecs were the overlords, but the city was Mayan through and through.

The cult of human sacrifice became very important to the ex-barbarians and all their conquered lands. The ritual of the ceremonial murders of earlier days was expanded. The infamous Sacred Well is at Chichén Itzá, where young men and women were thrown into the well as a way of giving them to the gods. If they lived after the fall, they were hauled out and asked if there were any messages from the gods.

In 1160 Tula was destroyed by new invasions of Chichimecs. After the Toltec leaders and their armies were driven away from their old capital and pushed southward, they took over the cities of less powerful chiefs when they could. They built new fortified cities when held off from other towns. From these new Toltec centers they fought the barbarians as they raided in the south.

Some of these newer cities even began to prosper. No general union was attempted, but single cities did show that civilization had not vanished after the fall of Tula.

Mitlá, a city built by some of the earliest Chichimec invaders, the Mixtecs, reached a high point in Middle American culture. During a time of constant warfare, 1160–1350, the Mixtecs built a small kingdom around themselves, and included the ancient center at Monte Albán. They were efficient governors and kept the peace, growing very rich in the process. One of the largest collections of jewels and art objects ever found belonged to Mixtec princes. Gold, silver, turquoise, and jade jewelry that required elaborate handwork was designed by Mixtec craftsmen.

The barbarian wars came to an end with the settling

of the third invasion of Chichimecs. A civil war, a struggle between the cities, began after that. From the beginning of the thirteenth to the end of the fourteenth
centuries, first one city and then another tried to take
over the rule that Tula had held. Each king or chief
tried to build up his farmlands and his city walls and
then take over other cities. There were vigorous, rich
cities in every valley in Middle America at that time.
The lake regions were particularly prosperous, par-
tially because of a new type of farming that had grown
up in Mexico.

Artificial garden islands called chinampas were built
on the lakes or around them. The Chinampaseros cut
canals through the rotting lake vegetation and in the
swamplands near the lakes; mud and compost from the
canal bottoms were piled on each side of the canal, and
crops were planted on the islands.

A Chinampasero could raise four crops a year on his
land. The soil never wore out, for fresh mud could
always be hauled up from the bottoms of the canals.
The islands grew higher and higher, and new islands
were started from old ones. It was very important to
the growth of the cities to have such large crops come
from such small plots. The cities faced the same problems as the earlier centers: population limitation
because there was no way to import food efficiently.
Thus the chinampas were a good solution.

The Aztecs, one of the last of the wild Chichimec
warrior bands to invade Mexico, built their prosperity
on the chinampas of Lake Texcoco. The Aztecs had
been even more primitive in their life-style than other
Chichimec tribes. They were still cave dwellers when
the Mixtecs were making gold filigree. The Aztec cave
site in the north is called Aztlan. The people took their

tribal name from it just before A.D. 1200, when they invaded.

The Aztlans, or Aztecs, had one very important god named Huitzilopochtli, the Left-handed Hummingbird. A left-handed hummingbird does not sound like anything that would inspire fear, but this hummingbird was no god of flowers, gardens, and nectar. He was a god that demanded a constant supply of human victims to be sacrificed to him. He made the old gods of human sacrifice, Xipe Tolec and Tezcatlipoca, look like tales from the Amerind equivalent of Mother Goose.

A wooden figure of Hummingbird was carried around by the wandering Aztecs. Hummingbird was wrapped in cloth and taken out only to be consulted by his priesthood.

The Aztecs raided and warred until they finally got the right to settle on lands near the old Toltec city of Culhuacán. The ruler of Culhuacán at that time was a king named Coxcox. He tolerated the Aztecs and even treated them as allies. He gave his daughter to Aztec ambassadors when they asked for her because he believed that she was going to become the wife of the Aztec chief. This family tie, he believed, would help the two peoples remain on good terms.

The Aztec priests worried about their own power if a strong alliance were made with Coxcox. They killed the girl and then invited her father to come to their temple to see what they had done. The priests knew that it would cause war. Coxcox, horrified by the death of his daughter, declared war on the whole Aztec tribe. Leading his armies against the Aztecs, he drove them into the marshlands of Lake Texcoco, where they were cut off from their villages and farms. There he thought they would be helpless.

Once the tribe was outlawed, the Aztec priesthood was in full power again. The priests declared that the lake was just the place that Hummingbird had been looking for to make a permanent home. Hadn't the god advised his priests to look for a place where an

The warrior farmer
who was the backbone of the
Aztec army

eagle who was eating a snake stood on a rock beside a cactus? Hadn't the priests seen an eagle like that on an island in the lake?

The whole valley of Mexico, including the Lake Texcoco area, is full of rocks, cactuses, eagles, and snakes, so it was not hard for the priests to prove their point with any number of sightings.

The Aztecs settled down on the islands in Lake Texcoco and laid claim to much of the marshland. Having learned about chinampas farming on their earlier travels, they began to build these fertile islands on the lake. There they were safe from their enemies and soon had an ample food supply.

Settling down did not make the Aztecs any gentler. They continued raiding their neighbors around the lake for slaves, art goods, women, and sacrificial victims. Hummingbird collected the hearts of thousands of captives.

The city of Tenochtitlán was planned and built by the Aztecs on Lake Texcoco. Its streets were canals. Buildings and temples in the city were the grandest that Mexico had ever seen. All the technical skills of stone-cutting and pyramid-building were learned from the people around them or from the slaves. They adopted not only the crafts but, gradually, the scholarship of the past. The written language that had started with the Olmecs, the calendar of the Maya, and the arts and sciences of two thousand years of Middle American history were taken over as the Aztecs extended their state.

Still, everything governmental was coated with the violent traditions of their own past.

After a century of settled life, social customs softened, at least. Aristocratic young people were taught refined manners as well as military zeal. Some of the refinements were almost Oriental: flowers were held in a certain way; graceful gestures were used in polite conversation; poetry and music were studied. Tenochtitlán became the shining city of art and learning as well as the center of military power.

Early in the fifteenth century there were more than 300,000 people in Tenochtitlán. Great pyramids and temples stood in the central square of the city. Schools for boys who would be soldiers, priests, and civil servants were nearby. Marketplaces had permanent shops. Fine houses for wealthy religious leaders, generals, and merchants were part of the city.

The high priests conducted more and more terrible ceremonies of human sacrifice. Wars had to be almost constant to supply enough victims. Kings saw their own power increasing with the priests' demands, so they conducted wider and bloodier campaigns until Monteczuma II.

Monteczuma became king in 1502. From the beginning the young Aztec ruler was an intellectual who questioned the ways of the temple. He studied the legends of Topiltzin, the gentle Toltec. While admiring the past, he also had more modern concerns. One was the place of religion in men's lives. Monteczuma did not fit the cruel Aztec mold at all. But it was too late for his opinions to matter.

In early Pueblo times pottery took over basket functions

IMPERIALISM AND DIVERSITY: *11*

The North American West

The rich culture of Middle America continued to influence many parts of the north. There may have been less contact with the deserts of the Southwest than there had been during the Culture Bridge era. The strong Chichimec tribes may have discouraged trade or travel between the Valley of Mexico and the Arizona-New Mexico communities. Corn-growing had given an early kind of unity to all people of the Tortilla Basket. But after that the North American desert tribes developed more independently.

By the tenth century A.D. the Anasazi Basket Makers had given up all their foraging ways and had become full-time farmers. They built villages, pueblos, out of their primitive settlements. Pueblos sprang up on the tops of mesas and along the edges of canyons.

Houses were built of stone with adobe mortar. These houses grew larger and larger and included more and more small rooms. The style of the little pit houses was not completely abandoned. They became the kivas, the sacred chambers. Probably it was because they were the oldest kind of building. The kivas in even the biggest pueblos were very much like the older pit houses—but on a grander scale. Kivas were usually round, with a hole in the roof for an entrance. They held all the religious objects of a particular cult and seem to have been used as men's clubhouses, too. In a place like the pueblo apartment, where people lived close together, such a club might be a necessity—to the women as well as the men.

The Anasazi civilization was at its height in the eleventh century. In places like Chaco Canyon great apartment houses were built; one, Pueblo Bonito, housed about 1,500 people. Until the end of the nineteenth century there was no other multiple dwelling unit in the Western Hemisphere so large.

Farms had to be watered by extensive irrigation. There was enough water to fill the ditches and reservoirs in these times. Bumper crops filled the storage baskets in the adobe storehouses. There was little sickness in the clean, dry air. In about 1050 the pueblos provided one of the most pleasant life-styles in the Americas.

Some pueblos were built into cliffs. The Cliff Dwellers of southern Colorado were just another pueblo people who were using their area to their best advantage. The desert-foraging, data-processing skills continued as one of the strong talents of the people. The cliff pueblos of Mesa Verde were made of stone fitted into the old caves and rock formations.

The people of the different pueblos had many things in common. Their languages, their religion, and their ways of living were not exactly alike, but all were similar. There was no network of temple centers. Indeed, there were no temples at all. Worship centered on the many kivas and special religious days. There were religious customs, like prayers, that were observed several times a day. The pueblos were alike, too, in having rigid rules of behavior—of great importance where so many people lived closely together.

Kiva and native Southwest inhabitant

Each pueblo developed its own style of pottery and cloth designs, with wares traded between pueblos. Turquoise objects were especially desired. Turquoise had become the holy stone because it was the sky's color.

At one time scientists believed that the pueblo people were peaceful. Their lives, centered on the kiva, seemed so orderly that it was assumed they did not have much to quarrel about. But after a close look at pueblo life, investigators found that the pueblo people were anything but peaceful.

Every pueblo had its war shaman as well as shamans

who worried about rain, wind, and stars. The people were always ready for war, and they seem to have fought often. The mistake about the peacefulness of the pueblos was made because we often think of war in terms of territorial gain for the victor. But that must not have been the motive for fighting. The pueblos grew by cells, not square miles and they may have fought one another for goods or water rights.

The pueblos also fought the Athabascan people, the Navajo and the Apache. These tribes were descended from Pacific rim peoples who came to the Western Hemisphere after A.D. 900. They appear to have been nomadic seafaring people at first, but they moved far inland in the Americas. They must have seemed far cruder to the pueblos than the wildest Chichimec seemed to the Teotihuacanos. The fact that they held out at all against these Athabascans shows that the pueblos could defend themselves very well.

Warfare may have been responsible for draining the energies of the pueblos. Perhaps the fields were neglected and the essential irrigation ditches allowed to build up silt. Then the drought came.

The time between A.D. 1276 and 1296 was a spell of extremely hot, dry weather. It affected the pueblos from Nevada to Texas. Rivers dried up or changed course, and the great pueblo of Mesa Verde was abandoned. Other smaller pueblos held out, but they supported fewer and fewer families.

The great days of the Pueblo culture were over.

There is another possible reason for the decline of the pueblos. Scientists now believe that profound social problems arise when people live as close together as they did in the pueblos. The rules of behavior have to be very strict. People still had quarrels, and families

Kachina, part of Pueblo religion

Style of Chaco Canyon
Pueblo pottery

feuded. Studies of modern-day pueblo people show that they often suffer from these same problems. If people do not have sufficient space, their individualism suffers and their humor turns to bitterness.

The tribes who have descended from the ancient pueblos—peoples like the Hopi, Zuñi, Taos, San Ildefonso, and Isleta—have tried to solve their social problems and still maintain the desirable elements of that life-style. Pueblo cooperation is a thing not many ancient people developed at all.

The people north and west of the Pueblo were the Shoshone. They may have been the last of the real scroungers left in North America. In South America tribes like the Yahgans still scrounged for a living a few years ago.

The Shoshone had no settlements, not even temporary ones. They did not try to build huts along the trails. They slept under bushes or accepted the protection of a rock pile. Their tools had not developed into anything specialized enough for hunting or foraging. They had no way of preserving or storing food even if they had a surplus. But there seldom was anything left over, for their scrubland was the worst in the Great Basin.

The Shoshone were spread out thinly over the most uninhabitable parts of Utah, Idaho, Colorado, and eastern California. There was never enough food in any

Early Apache sighting arrow for straightness

place to support more than a small population, usually one family and its near relatives. These tiny bands were on the move constantly.

The scrubland was not reliable enough for a foraging calendar, even if the people had wanted to try another kind of life. Deserts are hot and dry, but the climate is something that can be counted on. In the Shoshone lands in the Basin there were droughts, storms, and destructive winds that shifted the animal populations and altered the vegetation. Roots, grasshoppers, rabbits, and an occasional antelope filled the people's stomachs.

The Shoshone found out how to make nets from their neighbors, but they learned nothing about milling the hard seeds into flour in those early times.

The Ute, Paiute, Shoshone, and Gosuite tribes were the Shoshone who survived into modern times. The European settlers who met them were unable to understand their life-style. Only recently have scientists begun to appreciate that it takes skill and often great courage to wring a living from the land as the Shoshone did.

East of the Shoshone basin lands were the tribes of the Great Plains. These tribes were changing their way of living toward the end of the period and they were doing it in an unusual way. First the plains tribes learned to farm, and then they became—of all things—hunters!

The Great Plains had recovered their grasses sufficiently to attract game. The sun still turned the ground cover to the driest hay in late summer, but winter snow and rain gave enough moisture to support the new growth. Many types of grasses returned. They carpeted the land from the eastern woodlands to the dry Great Basin.

Mandan earth lodge

Bison migrated to the plains in great numbers. The new bison was a variety that could stand the cold winters and hot summers better than a cousin that continued to live in the woodlands. The plains bison spread out across the grasslands, and a new ecological pattern developed. Its main elements were grass, bison, wolves, and—later—man.

Tribes of Amerinds moved west onto the grasslands, too. There is no reason to think that it was because of the bison. They were Midwest farmers. They settled near or among the plains foraging people and went right on farming. The old foraging population learned plant cultivation, too.

People like the Mandan settled in the northern plains. They lived in villages of earth lodges. The lodges were built with poles and heaped sods, very much like the ones the white settlers made when they came to the plains. Tribes like the Wichita and Pawnee were in the southern plains. They had grass houses.

The tribes did a little hunting along with their farming after they settled the plains. They may not have gone on more than one bison hunt every year, when the herds were close to their villages. They took just enough bison to give them meat and to supply them with hides, bone, and sinew. They used the bison in about the same way that their woodland ancestors had used deer. The older plains foraging population may originally have sought out some bison, but they were not organized for herd hunting, either.

Hunting bison on foot was a tricky business. The people learned to disguise themselves in wolfskins because they found out that a bison herd ignored a few prairie wolves. The hunters, in their disguises, could get close to the bison and then spear the animals or shoot them with arrows. They also hunted by setting fire to the plains grass and by driving the bison over the cliffs the way the Iec Age hunters had once done with mammoths.

The bison were cut up into small pieces and loaded on pairs of poles that were dragged by big dogs. The French called this device a travois. In winter, the dogs pulled toboggans instead of the travois.

A Plains travois

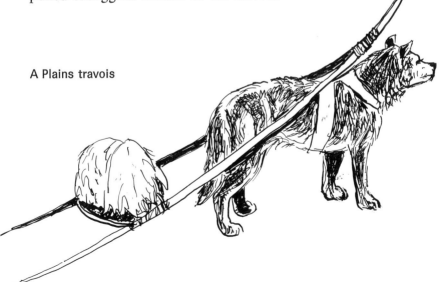

As the bison multiplied rapidly on the plains, the hunting life became more and more attractive. The tribes went on longer and longer hunts. They went out to meet the bison instead of waiting for them to come near the villages. Bison made up the plains diet a larger part of each year, and, since the bison-hide tipi could be taken down and moved easily, it came into general use. The tribes still maintained their village centers, but in the centuries just before the white man arrived, the farmer began to cultivate less and hunt more.

One of the reasons for the decline in the farming life was harassment from the Navajo and Apache, those same Athabascans who were raiding the Pueblo. The Navajo and Apache followed the bison herds for a living. In their contacts with the settled plains tribes they learned how to cultivate corn, and some raised crops as a secondary occupation. But they continued to be aggressive and warlike.

The increasing bison herds set the pattern. Plainsmen, immigrants or ancient inhabitants, were turning their backs to the settled life in the sixteenth century.

In the Far West, beyond the Shoshone scroungers, the foraging life still prevailed. There were exceptions, however. A few southern California tribes—the Diegueno, Mojave, Yuma, and Kamia—grew corn. These people were relatively close to the Pueblo and influenced by them. They spent very little time away from their fields.

Desert foragers, like the Wintun and Cahuilla in California, made the acorn serve the way corn served the farmer.

Acorns cannot be eaten without processing. Even the scroungiest scrounger can't digest a raw acorn. Acorns have a very high tannic acid content. Tannic acid is very good for curing hides, but it is not very good for human stomachs. The foragers ground their acorns on milling stones. The ground acorn mush was laid on sand and boiling water was poured over it.

Water was boiled in baskets in many of the California desert foraging areas, as it was in other places in North and South America. A tight basket was filled with water. Hot stones were dropped into it. The water boiled.

The boiling water washed out the acid, which drained into the sand. The acorn meal that remained on top

Boiling by dropping hot stones in water-filled basket

was pressed into cakes. They could be baked into acorn bread. It was a long process, making acorn bread out of the harvested acorns. It was done for thousands of years in California, from the time of the Oak Grave people, who were Adaptive foragers, until modern times.

One of the best organized foraging peoples in the Far West was the Pomo. The Pomo built a culture on the land around the old Borax Lake site. Their basket weaving marked one of the peaks in that art. For example, one kind of Pomo basket was made with feathers. The people used the reeds of the lake to make houses, baskets, and boats. Canoes made of these reeds did get waterlogged, but they could be hauled out of the lake and dried easily.

The Pomo were developing rapidly about 1600. They showed signs of becoming a tribe of some commercial importance, having a form of money made of clamshells and a counting system based on fours.

The forested coast begins in northern California and continues to the Arctic tundra. The Athabascan invaders, finding it much to their liking, became the dominant people along the coast.

Northwest coast culture, which was at its height when the white man came, was based on the bounty of the ocean, the beach, the rivers, and the cedar tree. The ocean gave up porpoises, halibut, cod, candlefish, and nutritious seaweed. Clams and crabs could be harvested on the beach; the rivers provided salmon; the prairies provided the rich camas root. Cedars were used for canoes, houses, and the totem poles that distinguished the tribes of the Northern forests from the Atlantic to the Pacific. Cedar bark was even twined and twisted and shredded to make rope and clothing.

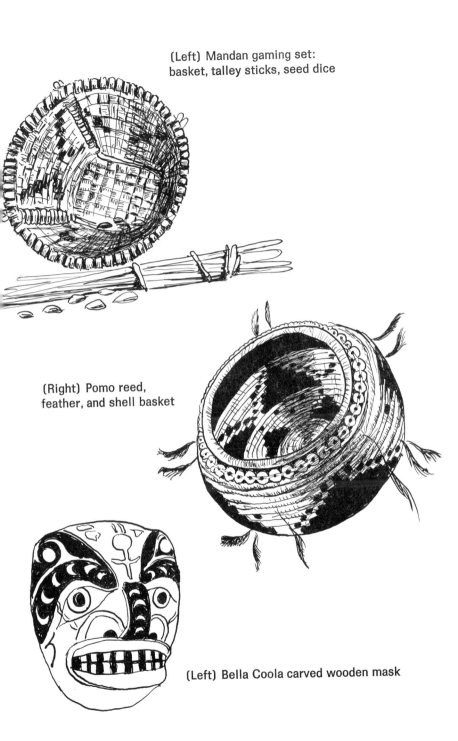

(Left) Mandan gaming set:
basket, talley sticks, seed dice

(Right) Pomo reed,
feather, and shell basket

(Left) Bella Coola carved wooden mask

The architecture of the Northwest coast people was totally different from anything else in the Americas. It was more like the building style of Polynesian ceremonial houses than anything in the Western Hemisphere. It is considered to be more evidence of the Pacific origins of the Athabascans. The coast people used the houses for festivals as well as for living. The houses, square or rectangular, had gabled or sloping roofs. A small one might measure 20 by 30 feet; a big one could be 500 feet long. The framework was upright cedar posts and crossbeams which were sheathed with split cedar and faced with cedar planks. There were two openings, a door in the side and a smokehole in the roof. During the warm months the people lived on the beach, and during the cold wet months around Seattle there is not much reason for windows.

Canoes were made from whole trees, hollowed out with fire. A Northwest canoe, like a Northwest house, was totally different from the product of the eastern woodland tribes. The delicate birchbark canoe of the Ohio River could have been crushed like a toothpick by the Northwest version, which often was 60 feet long and propelled by eighty paddlers.

The foragers of the Pacific Northwest coast counted their wealth in woven blankets, dried salmon, oil, fine baskets of spruce and cedar, wooden chests, wood carving, and slaves. They became so rich that they developed the peculiar ceremony known as the potlatch. At a potlatch rich men competed with one another to see who could give away or destroy the greatest number of possessions. Unfortunately, this display of waste included the slaughter of slaves. It was a unique kind of sacrifice, not to appease an awful god, but a kind of

Northwest seagoing canoe

economic boasting. There were signs that the killing of the slave captives, as a practice, was waning. There really was not much need for war, and there was no strong leadership, religious or military, to press for ritual murders. Tribal government was weak in the Northwest; individuals were strong.

Some of the coastal people were whalers. The Makah, Quinault, and Quileute went far out into the ocean to harpoon whales as they migrated up and down the coast. Whale products, such as whale oil, were much in demand. They could always be traded.

There was a bustling trade all along the north coast, even between its southern tribes and the fierce northerners, the Kwakiutl, the Tsimshian, and the Haida. The tribes spoke many different languages. Barter might have been a problem if a special trade language had not developed. In the absence of one dominant tribe—none of them would ever have admitted another was the leader—they used the Chinook jargon. It was used by the coast people, the river people, and the Plateau tribes far to the east of them.

On the California coast Hupa, Chumash, Costanoan, and Miwok collected from the sea and the open, hilly country behind them. They lived in large, densely populated villages that had all the advantages of a mild climate and a bountiful food supply.

The Chumash of the Santa Barbara coast are a good example of a rich Amerind culture that was based on foraging instead of agriculture. The Chumash were more than ordinary fishermen. They were seamen whose vessels would have been admired by any mariner. Since there were no stands of big trees near the Chumash, they built their big canoes of driftwood planks. It isn't an easy job to split planks from driftwood, even today. The Chumash did it with flint tools, and they made holes in the planks through which they threaded tule fibers to tie the planks together. The canoe was calked with the beach asphalt that still oozes black gum over the beaches.

Chumash art products rival those of the pueblos or Middle American cities. Besides the decorated canoes, there was beautiful carving done on wood and soapstone. Chumash houses had room partitions and four-poster beds.

The weather was mild, and food from the sea never failed them. About the only thing they had to fear was the huge California grizzly, now extinct, which had a great influence on the art and religion of the coast.

The Plateau tribes north of the scrounging Shoshone and east of the coastal foragers kept up the plains type of foraging that had gone on since Marmes Man in the Ice Age. Although their lands were dry, they were considerably more fertile than those of the Shoshone.

The Plateau tribes fed on salmon, deer, and elk in season; roots and berries were abundant. Villages were not permanent, but seasonal, and located in about the same spots each year. In summer the women made grass houses; in winter they covered the dry grass with woven mats to keep out the Plateau winds. Buckskin clothing, rabbit-fur blankets, and lined moccasins kept them warm.

Yakima, Nez Perce, Umatilla, Cayuse, Klicitat, Nespelem, Coeur d'Alene and Okonogan lived simply on the Plateau. They were near the Great Plains farmer hunters. Occasionally the young Plateau men would go out for big game on the plains and after a while they began to develop a taste for bison.

Temple Mound art: diorite bowl

(Left) Shell jewelry shows warlike spirit: one hand of main figure holds severed head

Iroquois war ax, mask, war club

IMPERIALISM AND DIVERSITY: 12

The North American East

Mound-building had not run its course with the death of the Hopewell culture.

The Mississippi Valley entered a period of concentration on mound-building. There were burial mounds in the south as early as 1000 B.C., but they were small and few before Middle America began to influence the Southeast. It was the Toltecs who set the Mississippians off on a building spree. Toltec traders or, possibly, immigrants carried Mexican ideas north and east. The valley started to show this influence about the same time that the Mexicans visited parts of Florida and settled the Caribbean islands in the eleventh century A.D.

The Temple Mound culture was not entirely Middle American. Like the Hopewell-Adenas, the Temple Mound builders of the Mississippi established their villages near rivers. One of the richest river basins in the world was tilled for the first time. The population exploded. There were 383 villages which scientists have counted along one 700-mile stretch of the Mississippi, and there were hundreds more on other parts of the big river and its tributaries.

The mounds which were the center of each village show Mexican design: huge and pyramid-shaped, with a wooden temple on top. The temples were destroyed at the end of certain ritual periods, and a new mound and temple were built on top of the old ones. Ramps or steps led up the sides of the pyramid.

The art objects, especially the ceramic pieces, which have been found in the Temple Mounds were often Toltec Mexican. They were either imported or very good imitations. Temple priests were dressed in a similar fashion to Toltec Mexican priests, even to the tips of their feathered headdresses. Human sacrifice was another similarity, though it was not necessarily an imported idea.

The Temple Mound builders contributed original ideas to Amerind culture. Though their society was based on classes, these were not castes as in the Toltec lands. The Natchez tribe, descendents of the Temple Mound builders, had a class system much like theirs. The Natchez chief was known as the Sun; there was an upper class whose members were referred to as "Suns;" and there was at least one large lower class. In order to be noble, or a "Sun," a Natchez tribal member had to have a mother who was a Sun and a father who came from the lowest social class. Once he was born noble, a man had to marry in the lowest social class again if he wanted his children to inherit his rights. This system was a way of enforcing social movement.

The soldier was an important person in Mound Builder society. A man could rise in the classes by performing well in battle.

Temple Mounds were still being built and used in the sixteenth century. By that time, however, most of the larger mounds had been abandoned, and a blight had fallen on the old civilization.

The chief heirs of the Temple Mound people were

the Natchez, Creek, Choctaw, Shawnee, Chickasaw, and Cherokee.

The old strongholds of the Hopewell-Adena were in crumbling ruins when the Mississippians were prospering. The people, living in small villages, were farmer foragers. Though they continued to be river people, they were on a path of cultural diversity that had begun at the end of Hopewell times. Nevertheless, they had some similarities. All grew corn or gathered wild rice, kept dogs, made pottery, used bows and arrows, and hunted the white-tail deer. Yet there were many differences as each family of tribes developed its own specialties.

The climate of the Midwest was still changeable. There was a warm spell from A.D. 1000 to 1300 around the Great Lakes, which may have encouraged migration to the area. The Midwest population increased to the point that wars were fought for territories—first between various cultural groups, and later between tribes that had developed from these cultures.

One of the important tribes that evolved was the Chippewa, who lived on the shores of the Great Lakes. In A.D. 1500 they were the largest distinct tribe north of Mexico. They controlled, or fought for, all the territory between Lake Huron and the Dakotas, pressing hard on the Dakotas to extend farther west. The war pipe was smoked much more often than the peace pipe was offered to an enemy of the Chippewa. Any tribal leader could send tobacco to another Chippewa village as a sign that he wanted allies for a raid. If the tobacco was accepted, the sender provided a feast at which the allies discussed their war plans.

Hunting, harvesting of wild rice, and visiting were done by canoe. The Chippewa were master canoe builders, using pliable birch bark instead of tree trunks for their craft. The birch bark was held inside a form which was made of stakes hammered into the ground. Ribs of bent cedar were placed inside the birch bark hull, and spruce gum was used to calk the canoe so that it would be watertight. The Chippewa canoe was considerably more navigable than the heavy dugout on the rivers.

Before 1600, tribes that later became horsemen of the plains lived in the Midwest. The Dakota were west of the Chippewa. The Cheyenne and Arapaho were Minnesota farmers. The Omaha, Osage, Kansa, Iowa,

Chippewa accepts war alliance by smoking gift tobacco

Kiowa, and Comanche and the ancestors of the Crow were living east of the Mississippi. And east of them were the Fox, Sauk, Menominee, and Miami, who had very little knowledge of the drama that was beginning in the grasslands.

East of the Great Lakes were the Huron and Iroquois, who had a common ancestral culture even after Hopewell times but who became bitter enemies.

The Iroquois people derived from several cultures of old Mound Builder people. They moved eastward during this period and formed themselves into a nation in present-day New York State. Algonkian foragers were already there when the Iroquois settled down, in good Midwestern fashion, along the riverbanks.

The Iroquois villages were permanent settlements, unlike those of their Algonkian neighbors. The Iroquois built rectangular longhouses, one for each large family group in the village. A log fence was erected around the houses and the storage buildings, and a belt of land was cleared around the village. The cleared lands were used for the corn and squash gardens that fed the village.

Corn, garden plots, the rights to the children, the rights of inheritance, most of the personal property, and most of the positions of importance in the early Iroquois tribes belonged to women. But this fact did not make the tribes any less warlike. They fought their traditional enemies, the Huron, to the west, as well as the Algonkians who raided their gardens. They conducted wars for new territories if they wanted some choice river or lake site where the foragers were camped.

In 1570 the five Iroquois tribes—Mohawk, Oneida, Onandoga, Cayuga, and Seneca—formed a union called the Hodesaunee. A man named Hiawatha, who was an official of the league, traveled all over Iroquois country getting support for the Hodesaunee from the five tribes. The union was one of the attempts to reverse the cultural diversity that was growing in the North.

The Iroquois fought fiercely when they made war and were known for their cruelty to captives. Yet in other ways they were an advanced people. They understood things about mental illness that were not common knowledge in medicine until the twentieth century. They knew, for instance, that people sometimes try so hard to forget unpleasant things that they become sick, and they believed that dreams were man's subconscious fears and wishes, not magical experiences.

Algonkian tribes occupied the subarctic forestland and the Atlantic coast as far south as Virginia. These were the people the Norsemen met about A.D. 1000. The Norsemen called them Skraelings and made uncomplimentary remarks about their appearance; but the Norsemen, with their yellow beards and hairy bodies, must have appeared equally ugly to the Amerinds.

The Algonkians were amazed by the Viking iron tools and the strange-looking animal that the Vikings unloaded from their ship. It was a bull that had been brought along to start a herd in Vinland, but there was not a single cow in the Americas. So the Vikings must have been disappointed on that score—though they were impressed by the fields of grain grown by the coast Algonkians, who were part-time farmers.

Tribes of the North Atlantic coast—Mohegan, Algonkian, Narragansett, and Delaware—were descendants of these coastal foragers who had found out about corn planting. Perhaps they had learned it as early as Hope-

Viking and Amerind exchange goods

well-Adena times. It changed their lives less than it did those of other Amerinds in the north, for corn was not essential to them. They dug clams on the shore and caught fish. There were a few attempts by these Algonkian peoples to form unions, but none lasted long.

A Calusa warrior

South of the Algonkians along the coast were tribes quite different from those who had learned farming by 1300. Later this area was settled so densely by Europeans that most of the Amerind history has been lost, and tribal names have even been forgotten.

One tribe that no one forgot, however, was the Calusa, who foraged the southern Florida peninsula in small bands. They knew about corn planting, but they didn't do much of it. They hunted, fished, gathered, and fought. The Calusa were powerfully built people, whose size and cruelty to captives gave them a fearful reputation on the coast. They were fine fishermen and took fleets of canoes out into the ocean as well as on the inland lakes and rivers. Cuba was one of their ports of call.

The Caribbean Sea had become a Mexican lake in Toltec times. The islands were populated by many Mexican immigrants, who kept in touch with the homeland for centuries. Canoes were going back and forth between Middle America and the islands when the white man came.

Athabascan snowshoe maker

IMPERIALISM AND DIVERSITY: *13*

The North American North

The cold forest was still the domain of the woodland hunter forager. Plant cultivation was probably known, but a tribe would have been foolish to depend on it, for the growing season was much too short. The Algonkians had perfected bows and arrows that enabled them to bring down the largest and the most elusive animals. In the southern part of their territory that animal was the moose; in the north it was the caribou.

The Athabascans may have come to the northwestern Canadian coast even earlier than they did to the northwest coast of the United States. The first immigrants may have begun filtering eastward about A.D. 600. Though they had been seamen, they could see the attractions of the rich woodland, and they came into Algonkian lands in greater and greater numbers. Gradually the eastern subarctic forest belonged to the Algonkian and the western part to the Athabascan.

Different tribes marked out their own hunting territories. Ojibway, Penobscot, Micmac, and Naskapi were the major Algonkian tribes. Yellow Knife, Chipweyan, Kaska, Slave, and Beaver were the Athabascan. Once in a while the tribes cooperated in hunting, but usually they kept to their own preserves.

The Algonkian and Athabascan, living under the

same conditions and having many contacts with each other, came to have very similar ways of doing things. Both used the portable skin wigwam, snowshoes, and toboggans, though all were probably Algonkian inventions, and they depended on the bow and arrow. Neither had religious centers like the people of the South.

Religion in the subarctic forest was centered on family gods, or totems. People showed their allegiance to a totem, usually an animal, instead of a temple god. The totems were often carved in wood and could be either large or small effigies. The totem pole was a family tree associated with a particular animal that was supposed to be especially vulnerable to hunters of a particular family. Frequently the animal had something to do with family beginnings. Tribesmen believed that families actually looked like their totems. For instance, a band of Penobscot that had a crab for its totem all looked a little crabby to other Penobscot who knew about the totem.

There was a practical reason for totems. They helped prevent intermarriages in territories where family connections might otherwise be lost. Except for totem likeness, closely related young people might marry, and their children could suffer from the kinds of diseases that come from parents who are too closely related.

The Alaskan Peninsula and the Aleutian island chain that stretches west of the subarctic forest were densely populated. There were probably 25,000 people living there in 1500. They were the Aleut branch of the Eskimo family, who still lived as sea-mammal hunters. Salmon and birds still filled out their diets, and there was always a supply of birds' eggs on the foggy cliffs. Blueberries, salmonberries, and starchy roots grew in the damp, mossy meadows of the islands. It was no wonder that a large population could be supported.

Whales were the most sought-after sea mammals. Men went out for them in two-man kayaks called bidarkas. The man in the prow carried a spear which had a slate tip smeared with aconite poison. Only the village shamans knew how to prepare the poison. When the hunters came close to a whale, the spear thrower plunged his spear into the whale's back. The aconite sickened the whale, which stayed close to the place where it had been hit and died within a few days. People in the villages waited for the whales to wash up on the beaches. Thus hunters might not get the same whale they had speared.

Aleuts used the atlatl and harpoon as well as the javelin type of spear. Aleut traditions were warlike and aggressive; they had slaves and lived by social castes. When they went to war, they wore rod armor. It was made of pieces of wood joined together with thongs. They also wore masks and wooden hats that were fastened to the armor with thongs.

The tribes of the Alaskan coast were afraid of the Aleuts. They fled when an Aleut war bidarka approached.

Aleutian villages were communities of pit houses called barabaras. A pole ladder was used to get down inside them, and the roofs were dry grass or sods laid over driftwood beams. Though they took a long time to dig, there were two reasons why the Aleuts bothered to do this. One was the wind that blows on the islands and along the peninsula, called the willawa, one of the strongest winds anywhere. The other reason was the lack of wood. There are no trees growing west of Kodiak; while driftwood is available, it is difficult to

Aleut whale hunters

use for complete structures. The barabaras were lighted by whale or seal oil, which doesn't produce much smoke.

The most famous art of the Aleuts was their basketry. Beautiful baskets were woven on all of the islands; on

Attu women went blind competing for the tiniest weave. Reed straw was put into a tub of water to soften it, and then the women split the silky straws into finer and finer strips with their fingernails. The thinner the strand, the tighter the basket. Aleut baskets were completely waterproof.

The Eskimos penetrated deep into the continent and claimed the tundra as well as the Arctic coast. Old tundra hunter sites likes Denbigh and Onion Portage show a mixture of tools after A.D. 600. Then the tools became Eskimo or Eskimo-like.

There is no indication of a struggle between the Eskimos and older Tundra hunters. There was no reason why there should have been. In a place where there is a constant battle against the elements, people may well regard one another as allies rather than enemies. Also, both groups of men sought wives. In the north country family groups are especially important; a lone man or woman has little chance of survival. A man who does not have a wife to prepare food, make clothing, and keep the fires burning is courting death. Equally, a woman must have a man to hunt food for her.

The Eskimos did fight the Athabascans. In the summer months the woodland caribou went onto the tundra to feed on the vegetation there, and the Athabascans followed. The Eskimo, regarding the tundra as his domain, fought fiercely for his barren world. Thus the two peoples became bitter enemies.

The Eskimos built new villages along the northern Arctic coast and west around the Seward Peninsula by the Bering Sea, the route of the first migrations, begun more than 50,000 years previously.

A totem pole

THE EUROPEANS 14

Many years ago the human population of the Western Hemisphere at the time of the European arrival was estimated to have been 15,000,000—a very sparse population for such a vast area. Today scientists believe that the Americas had many more inhabitants. Mexico alone may have had 37,000,000. South America was settled in every region. The Inca Empire supported 10,000,000 of these people. North America did not have so many people, but it too had its well-settled areas.

Growth had been slow. A handful of Ice Age immigrants had provided the seeds. It had taken 50,000 years and many more immigrants to grow the Amerind tree. The fending stick became the spear and the hard grain became flour without causing any great revolution on either continent. Potatoes were planted, and corn was cultivated. There was no sudden spurt out of the Stone Age into civilization. The roots of the tree inched down, and they went deep.

In 1500 it had only begun to bear fruit. It might have been fruit of great quality. It certainly would have been different from anything that grew across the Atlantic. The Old World was centered on a man who was proud to set himself apart from the rest of the natural world. But the Amerind had never been out of touch with the natural world. His cooperation and closeness with nature might have yielded something very profound in the way of civilization. But we never will know what might have happened. Monteczuma II never had his chance to recast the cruel Aztec religion even if he had planned to. The Spanish records show that he fell under a hail of stones his own people threw at him. The Mexicans say that Cortés had him strangled. Pizarro murdered Atahualpa, the last Inca ruler. In the north the process was slower, but it had the same effect. The corn cultivators, from Narragansett to Iroquois to Cherokee, were provoked, raided, and driven off their lands by the whites. The hunters were resettled where there was no hunting; the fishermen were pushed off the beaches. Even the scroungers were hounded away from their meager lands.

The European provided one gift for all he had taken. The Spanish horse came onto the plains. For one jubilant century, from the mid-eighteenth to the mid-nineteenth, another great Amerind culture flourished. The entire Great Plains took up herd hunting. The game was the bison, and he was hunted on horseback.

Tribes from totally different places and occupations took up the chase. The Dakota-Sioux, Crow, Cheyenne, Chippewa, Blackfoot, Arapaho, and the Athabascan Navajo and Apache came from the north and east. The Plateau Yakima, Cayuse, Nez Perce, Umatilla, and Okonogan came from the northwest. Comanche and some Shoshone arrived. The scrounging Ute and Piute became some of the best horsemen. The Kiowa took over the southern plain, along with the Pawnee.

At first there was pressure on the settled tribes—the Caddo, Pawnee, Wichita, and Mandan. Then they abandoned their old lives, restricted their pottery making, and took off after the bison.

They grew rich beyond their wildest dreams. Only the most desirable bison were taken—and with ease. There was so much meat that no one needed starve. Excess meat was dried in the sun for jerky or pounded together with berries for pemmican. Bison hide, meat, and horn could be traded to the white man. Tipis were filled with the products of the trading post. The herds of horses grew.

The feathered, painted tribes lost their allegiance to specific localities. They did not have to protect a particular game preserve or irrigated valley. But they fought anyway—for excitement, prestige, and horses. War became a game. Each player would expose himself to danger. Each tried to add up points for enemy dead. Counting coup—touching an enemy in combat—was the method of keeping score. Guns became important, and a plains armament race was carried on during the last forty years of the plainsmen's day. Yet it still was considered more important to kill an enemy with a spear. Personal achievement replaced family position or any kind of inherited wealth.

The dream faded fast. Before it had even begun, European settlers had turned west from the Atlantic coast. They had no more regard for the new empire on the Great Plains than they had had for the corn villages in the eastern woodlands. By the middle of the nineteenth century they did not even have to fight their own battles because an arrogant national government with an ambitious military arm made war on the plains Amerinds. When it was over, there was not an independent tribe left west of the Missouri.

The north country did not escape, either. The tribes of the subarctic forest were forced to strip the land of pelts for the customers of the British Hudson's Bay Company, while the Aleuts were brutalized by Russians from the east.

It seemed inevitable that the entire Amerind world would be destroyed.

Dust filled the pueblos.

Some white men felt a twinge of shame when they began to realize what they had done. They felt generous. They offered the Amerind brotherhood.

Sealth, the chief for whom Seattle was named, expressed one Amerind's opinion about this. He remarked that he could not see much resemblance between the two peoples. Then he reconsidered. When the white man's time of decay came, they might be brothers, after all.

It was a miracle that the Amerind did not become extinct. Like the true descendant of the scrounger who outlasted the glaciers, he survived.

The Europeans who took over his land understood practically nothing about the Amerinds' culture and heredity. During the past the white man of the Western Hemisphere has acted as if nature were an enemy. He has believed in unlimited growth, competition, and the right to vandalize the land. The earth as Amerind saw it, a closed system, was not a part of the invaders' tradition. The white man treated the land with even more contempt than he treated the human beings who inhabited it for so many centuries. It was only when the land grew sick, the streams poisoned, and the air polluted that the white man remembered a people who had managed it differently. Then he began to look more deeply into Amerind history to see if there might be clues to a happier relationship with nature.

The white man is searching, often with the help of modern Amerinds. In the face of a rebelling environment, a new bond has grown up between native and immigrant.

We may be brothers, after all.

Index

The Author

Since graduating from the University of Chicago, RUTH H. SHIMER has taught school in Illinois, Michigan, Arizona, the state of Washington, and on the Alaskan island of Unga, east of the Aleutians. Throughout her travels Mrs. Shimer has been an enthusiastic amateur archaeologist and has visited many important prehistoric Amerind diggings. Mrs. Shimer, her husband, Robert, and their two children live at present in Claremont, California.